Don't Get Screwed!

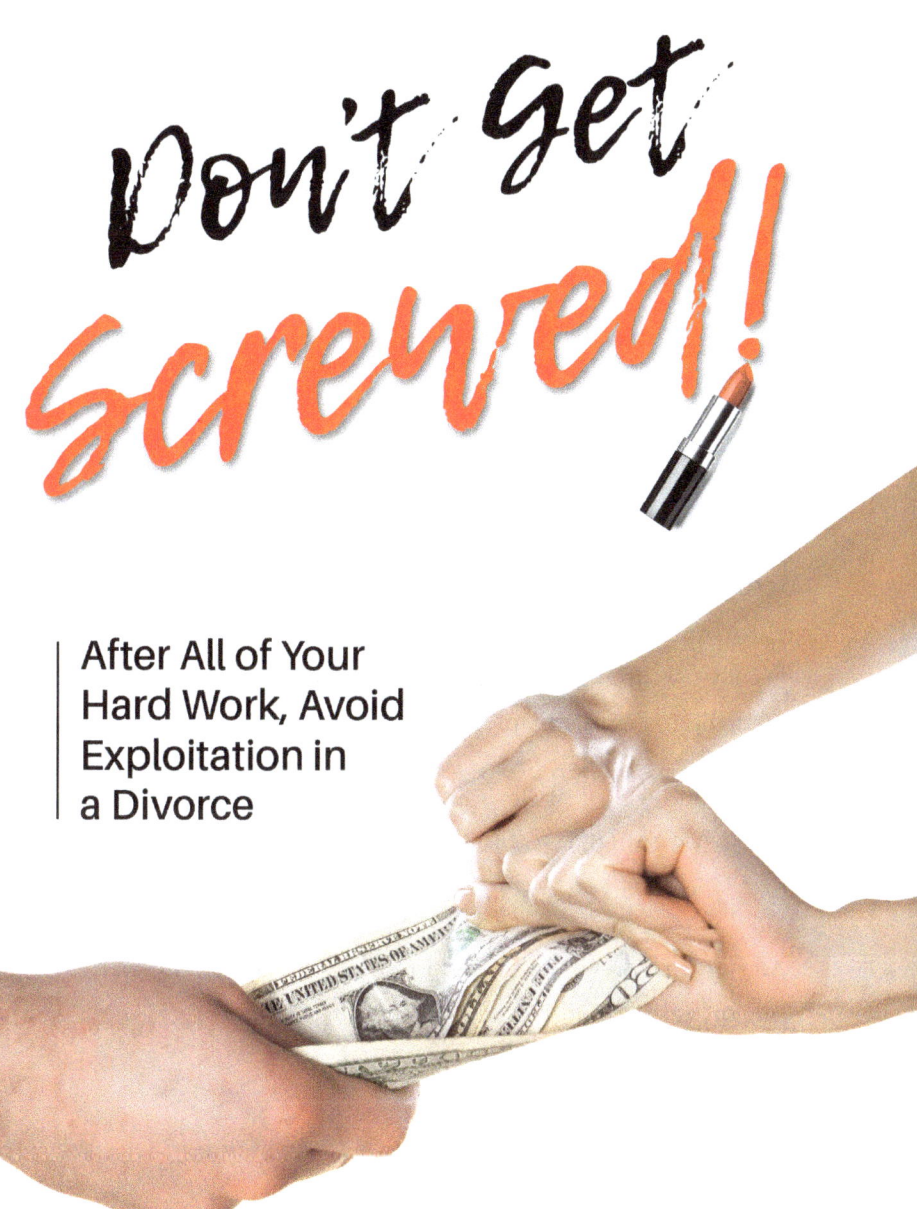

| After All of Your
| Hard Work, Avoid
| Exploitation in
| a Divorce

MICHAEL S. JOYNER, MD

No part of this publication may be reproduced, stored in a retrieval system, or transmitted in any form or by any means, electronic, mechanical, photocopying, recording, or otherwise, without written permission of the author. For information regarding permission, please contact the author.

ISBN: 979-8-9867716-0-1

All rights reserved. Published in the United States of America by Forever My Daddy LLC.

Dedication

Dedicated to

Love, Hope and Possibilities.

The love that my family and extended family has always had to share.

The hope that I have always had that my sons would want to get to know me.

The possibilities that could be.

Table of Contents

iii	*Dedication*
vii	*Introduction*
1	**CHAPTER ONE:** High-Value Targets
9	**CHAPTER TWO:** "The D-Word"
17	**CHAPTER THREE:** It Happened to Them, and I Could Happen to You
23	**CHAPTER FOUR:** Settlements and Asset Loss
35	**CHAPTER FIVE:** Alimony and Child Support
53	**CHAPTER SIX:** Loss of Custody and Parental Alienation
69	**CHAPTER SEVEN:** Co-Parenting
82	**CHAPTER EIGHT:** In Your Corner
91	**CHAPTER NINE:** Don't Be a Target
105	*Conclusion*
107	*Glossary*
115	*References*
119	*Acknowledgements*

Introduction

"The D-word." It's a worst-case scenario that nobody likes to think about. There's an enormous stigma surrounding divorce. Divorce is a horrible word! Most people associate the end of a marriage, however amicable it may have been, as a failure that reflects on them. Even though almost 45% of marriages will end in divorce, few couples rarely even consider signing a prenup.

For high-value individuals like athletes and doctors, this number is even higher. There is some evidence to suggest that the divorce rate in the NFL is as high as 80%. In some surgical residency programs, the divorce rate was 110%. That meant that people would come into the program married, get divorced, remarry, and then get divorced *again* by the time they completed the program.

Divorce is much more common for these high-value individuals because they have to be so dedicated to their jobs. I've heard a saying in my own profession: "Work is the mistress." If you're looking to advance your career to that kind of place, then you have to be willing to put that kind of work in to get there. That's just how it is. Some people either can't handle taking on that much or can't handle having a partner who does.

As a surgeon, I had to go through decades of education and training before I was able to take my first career job. These positions obviously bring more money and status to someone, but they also take a massive amount of time and energy out of the person. It can be hard to balance family life with a demanding career.

Unfortunately, divorce is also more common for these types of people because they can often become sought-after for marriage simply for their status in the first place. Some potential partners may look at that person only for what they can give them instead of for who they are as a person. When people get married for those wrong reasons, it's not surprising that the marriage is more likely to end in divorce.

This type of divorce tends to get especially ugly as well. If someone has married a high-value individual only for the lifestyle, they aren't going to want to give that life up when the marriage ends. They often feel like they are owed what the person has given them as a spouse. They think, *You aren't going to take that all from me now.* In the case of divorce, high-value individuals will get taken for everything they have if possible.

I've experienced this personally. When I got divorced, I was completely naive about how the whole thing worked. I thought that it was a straightforward process where we would be co-parenting advocates and the courts would just look at the numbers and make formulaic calculations to determine custody, asset split, and the monthly payments. I also thought that lawyers were your legal advocates. I was very, very wrong. Divorce is over a billion-dollar industry. Many people are making money as a result of this challenging process.

The courts are not objective. Of course they will deny this, but don't believe them. Lawyers will lie, cheat, and steal to win their case. I've seen it firsthand. At the time of my divorce, I was just transitioning out of my military career. I hadn't yet finished my medical training. I was lucky to even be making any money during my education at that point, even though it wasn't very much.

I also had two cars at the time. The first was the family car and the second was my commuting car to get to and from work. I gave up that main car in the separation, and just had the second car to drive around. This is the car I drove to get to the court dates.

This car was also a used Porsche. Not the fancy kind of Porsche that costs the same as a house. I couldn't afford anything like that. I was driving what they call "the poor man's Porsche," a 986 Boxster I had bought for $5,000. The car was only worth the fact that it could get me places. And when it couldn't, I ended up selling it for one whole dollar.

That didn't matter in the courtroom. To them, they used it to make me out to be some "rich doctor who drives a luxury sports car and isn't focused on his kids" when that couldn't be farther from the truth. They didn't want to know the truth. All they wanted was to take anything they could to twist it into making me the "Bad Guy" and making me pay. They want to portray fathers as "deadbeat dads" to get more money from them, and do not let anyone tell you otherwise. If you think differently when going into a courtroom, you will get screwed!

At the end of the day, that's all that they were after: money. I had this realization when I was sitting in a room with both of our attorneys as they made negotiations. I was paying both of them. My ex wasn't even there. It occurred to me then that the only reason the attorneys were there and doing all of this was because they thought I had money, and they thought that they could get some of it. That was really it. They did not care about my relationship with my kids. They did not care about how much quality time I would be able to spend with them. They cared about how much money went into her pocket—and theirs.

When I say that attorneys really are not your friend and how you can get seriously exploited in this process, I often hear this pushback: "Yeah, but what if the parent is a deadbeat? What if they're abusive?" Let me make it clear that these are not the kind of divorces that I'm talking about. When there is ever any criminal element, all of this gets thrown out the window. I'm referring only to the straightforward divorces where things just didn't work out. That is where the injustice is.

Though they may deny it, many attorneys don't really care about their clients, or the kids, or anything. The fact is they want to win their case, no matter what. And they want to get paid. Don't get it twisted, they are looking out for your best interests…as long as you pay them. The second they think you might not be able to, they're gone. I've had it happen to me before.

But the worst part of it was not the financial loss. For me, it was experiencing parental alienation. Before all of this, I didn't even know what the phrase was or what it meant. I had to learn it in the hardest way possible.

I believe my two sons were unfortunately used as pawns in our divorce. After all, they were the only two things I really cared about in all of this. This is true for many parents. I was denied access to my own children. It was the worst thing that I have ever experienced, and I wouldn't wish it on anyone. Even to this day, they have been so well-trained in the form of alienation that they deny me access to them as young adults. Parental alienation, unfortunately, works.

Time with your children is the absolute worst thing to lose in a divorce. Everything else—money, possessions, even mental peace—can eventually be replaced. Time is the one asset you can't get back. Time is absolutely essential to establishing a relationship with your children as well. If your children never get time to know you, then you can't ever really bond. There are so many children in the world who have lost out on relationships with a parent who wanted to be in their life but was prevented from doing so. That's so much unnecessary pain.

I kept a journal throughout my experience and struggles to get time with my sons. This journal later turned into my first book, *Forever My Daddy: Denied*. What was at first just a personal outlet for me surprisingly became a resource for other people going through the same thing.

By sharing my experience, I have been able to help others. I've been told that some people have been able to take the lessons that I had to learn personally and use them to better their own situation. To me, that has been what's given some meaning to my struggles. If anybody can get anything out of what I've been through, then it makes it all worth something.

I started to give lectures here and there after the publication of my first book. When coming out of these lectures, I'd occasionally have someone come up to me asking for specific advice. I'd give it to them, they'd go off, and then someone else would reach out asking for advice as well. One person would tell another to talk to me, that person would tell another person…and so on. I got pretty busy.

All of these organic referrals motivated me to make an established practice of advising others. I became a certified divorce coach so that I could legitimately advise others going through a divorce and mediate in difficult situations. However, I do not give legal advice and I am not a lawyer.

My goal is always to make the process as amicable and easy as it can be, keep everyone out of the courtroom as much as possible, and to help establish a healthy co-parenting relationship when children are involved. That is why I founded MJ MD Mediation, Coaching, and Sports Management.

My company has also expanded to offer sports management at my agency, Condition Sports Management. As a hand surgeon, inventor, and entrepreneur, I know what it takes to build a career as big as an athlete. I also know what it's like to be a high-value individual and how you can get targeted because of it. Being targeted and exploited in a divorce comes with the territory for a high-powered position like in sports. I want to especially help these young athletes learn how to navigate these potential issues, focus on their career, and then manage the transition when the game ends.

My goal for this book is to help high-value individuals keep what they've worked hard for in the case of a divorce by using both my personal experience and professional expertise to explain:

- What the "worst case scenarios" of a divorce are and why they can occur.
- How to prevent these situations from happening.
- Strategies to protect *all* of your assets: property, money, energy, and time.
- The people you need in your corner to get through the process while still focusing on your career.
- How to avoid becoming a target in the first place.

Divorce is always a possibility. It's going to happen to someone, somewhere. By taking some preventative measures and reducing the negative connotations that the event has, those experiencing it can strive to come out the other side as positively and with as little loss as possible.

Divorce appears more common for high-value individuals than the average population, especially since there are higher stakes involved. In this situation, they turn into targets for their ex spouse, the lawyers on both sides, and the courts to exploit them as much as possible. While divorce can happen to *anyone*, the possibility is especially high for these individuals. And if they haven't taken any asset protection measures, divorce can incur a greater loss than usual.

There's one reason for all of that: money.

CHAPTER ONE

High-Value Targets

High-value individuals are those who have accumulated a significant amount of wealth, fame, and/or status from advancing in their high-profile and high-paying careers. Most of the time, high-value individuals enjoy the many perks that come with their professional accomplishments. After all, they've earned it.

But there are real drawbacks, including a total lack of privacy, vulnerability to manipulation and exploitation, and the responsibilities that come with fame, wealth, and status. We've seen these drawbacks splashed across magazines and "news" outlets since the beginning of print media and with our technology today, maintaining privacy is virtually impossible.

For someone in this position, attracting materialistic and ill-intended people is inevitable. In an athletic career, it just comes with the territory. When forging new relationships, a high-value individual is left to determine whether a person is genuinely invested in their connection or if it's a ploy to gain fame or wealth. It's enough of a pattern that the term "gold digger" was developed specifically to describe those who seek out individuals for their own financial gain.

For decades, movies and books have portrayed a "gold digger" as a vivacious young woman seeking out an older, well-established, and wealthy man. These over-the-top depictions fall just short of quite literally spelling out what she's after. If only it were that obvious.

> ### Stop and Think
>
> It's not just a movie trope. How many times have you heard about a famous athlete or celebrity paying out in a divorce? How many people do you personally know who have been exploited by their ex for financial gains? This is a very real risk that all high-value individuals, regardless of gender, face.

Unfortunately, if you're a high-value individual, there's a whole queue of people lining up to exploit you for their own gain. They want your money, your fame, and whatever else they can get their hands on. And some people are very good at playing the part of the genuinely-in-love partner. Quite often, they can fool even those with a "radar" for being targeted. What you have to offer is no doubt going to be part of any partner's attraction. That makes sense. After all, everyone has to bring something to the table. But if that is the only thing they care about, then they definitely don't care about you: they only care about what you can give them.

Now, that kind of relationship might work for a while. But relationships based only on a one-sided benefit are much more likely to end. And when they do, that partner is often accustomed to what they've been given. They aren't going to let all that go so easily. This is when high-value individuals are hit the worst, and they may have never seen it coming. They may have never understood that they were in that kind of relationship. It's difficult to know who you can trust and who's looking to take advantage of you. That's why prenups are even more important for high-value individuals.

High-net worth people are especially targeted in divorce proceedings and making the right preparations could save them from paying away their fortune in alimony. Some ex-partners fight for outrageous settlements or request unrealistic alimony to maintain the standard of living they've become accustomed to. When this lifestyle is threatened, they respond with lawyers to collect "their due." Not every person seeks to marry for money, but even the ones who don't still won't want to return to their less lavish lifestyle. This can make the divorce proceedings messier and more contentious, leading to drawn-out negotiations that ultimately benefit the lawyers.

Like I've said, attorneys are not your friend. If they think you have any money, they are going to try to get it: through fees, a cut of a settlement, however they can. Sometimes they can prove to be worse than the ex themselves.

High-value individuals appear more at-risk during divorces than your average person. They've likely acquired assets and have a reputation that could be damaged if the divorce turns ugly. These put them at a disadvantage when divorcing from a partner. Money is a motivator for many people and when there's money on the line, people's true intentions and worst qualities are exposed.

Take a look at your attorney, for example. You want to hire an attorney who's able to protect your assets and get what you want from the divorce. But this comes at a cost, one that's more than financial. Most attorneys will do whatever it takes to win, and they'll get their hands dirty if they have to. The big motivator for them isn't your reputation or even your assets. It's the check you write to them for their work. And the more hours they spend on your case, the more money they make.

I realized that myself during my divorce. Our conversations and negotiations kept going in circles and I was frustrated—neither my ex-wife nor I were swimming in money, so why was it so complicated? I realized then that my attorney wasn't truly on my team, they were on their own team: win the case but make money while doing it. With my fancy degree and brand-name (albeit outdated) car, these attorneys thought I had more to offer financially than I actually did. I knew that if I couldn't keep paying them, they'd quit before the ink even dried on the check.

The more assets you have, the larger your settlement will be, unless protected by a prenup. Consider some of the wealthiest couples in the world who go through a divorce. When a scandal hits the news and one of these wealthy couples pursues a divorce, what happens when they do not have a prenup? In the case of one couple, they married before the corporate empire success, but this lack of asset protection cost a lot of money and shares. In this case, the spouse became one of the wealthiest women in the world following their divorce. Such a high-profile divorce may seem like an outlier, but there are many famous athletes who've fallen into this same situation: seeped in wealth and prestige during their career but left virtually penniless after retirement and divorce. Why is that so common? The life of a professional athlete is dotted with occupational hazards: overzealous fans, highly publicized social lives, and the vulnerability that comes with being in the limelight. Many athletes also come from an average-income family. So when they do make it big, some are unequipped for the sudden rush of attention and money. Because so many athletes do not have the necessary guidance and know-how to protect their finances, they become the biggest targets for people looking to take advantage of them.

> ### Stop and Think
>
> How many athletes have you heard of going bankrupt in retirement, even after making so much money during their careers? What were some of the causes? For many, it's typically a mismanagement of their funds or expensive divorce settlements.

In addition to these elements, an athlete's life consists of high-pressure events, long hours of training, and frequent time away from home. And that's all without including the illicit activities that their high-paying salaries can afford and that their stressful careers might tempt them to do. This lifestyle contributes to relationship tensions, which makes it unsurprising that professional athletes experience a higher divorce rate than the rest of the population, estimated between 60%-80% depending on the sport in question. Athletes have to navigate traditional relationship woes *plus* the added pressures of their occupation. You'll find that many athlete divorces become fodder for gossip columns, but there are a few exceptions of uneventful divorces.

For example, one retired athlete, famous for his career in the NBA and his shoe line, went through a divorce. He and his ex-spouse met before his NBA career took off and they'd already had a child by the time they were married. After 17 years of marriage and a period of separation in 2002, the couple officially divorced in 2006 in what they both described as an amicable and mutually respectful separation. The two did also have a prenup, which was likely a large factor in what appeared to be smooth divorce proceedings. The settlement granted his ex-spouse $168 million, a 7-acre estate, and custody of their three kids. The NBA star has since remarried, but the two seem to maintain a friendly, respectful relationship. This is the exception, and he still had to pay a lot.

There are more contentious divorce stories than I have room to include in this chapter. Creating a prenuptial agreement is a reasonable action for both partners to take before getting married. If a marriage starts to fall apart, then people should seek out divorce coaches. For the average person, a divorce coach serves as an advocate who's there for *you*, unlike your attorney who's there for the paycheck.

High-value individuals are even larger targets in divorces and as such, should invest in extra guidance from someone who's been through the process and understands the highly emotional conditions of divorce proceedings. I am uniquely qualified as someone who experienced a tumultuous divorce and has since become a certified mediator and divorce coach. The divorce process may be foreign to you, but exploring its components with an expert can ease the stress and defeat you're experiencing now.

CHAPTER TWO

"The D-Word"

We all spend a large portion of our lives building up assets to prepare for the future. Let's face it: American culture is focused on assets and it's how we measure success. So why *wouldn't* we want to protect these long fought-for assets when we get married?

The notion of a prenuptial agreement and asset protection is viewed as preparing for divorce. Everyone wants their marriage to last, but in a country where almost 50% of all marriages end in divorce, it's not practical to ignore the possibility of divorce happening. A prenup doesn't mean that you're expecting a divorce or that you're a failure if you do separate from your partner. It's simply a legal agreement that's made with a practical mindset.

Divorce in and of itself is not necessarily a *bad* thing, either. It's never really a pleasant experience, but it should not carry the stigma and reflect back personally the way that it often does. A lot of people tend to forget that getting married is basically a contract to become legally recognized partners and have all of the benefits that come with it: ease of filing taxes and owning property, health insurance, inheritance, the ability to make important decisions for the other if needed, etcetera. When two people decide that they no longer want to be together, a divorce is simply the process of ending that contract, deciding the division and logistics of property/assets/custody/etcetera, and then moving forward.

At least, that's the most objective definition of a divorce. The reasons behind the divorce are often what drives people to conduct themselves in a less-than-stellar fashion during this time. It's oftentimes impossible to avoid the "why" of the divorce and all of the feelings associated with it. If emotions and attachments were not involved, most would act a lot more reasonably than they do.

> ### Stop and Think
>
> Statistically, you and many other readers are likely to have already gone through the divorce or separation of your parents. Are you a child of divorce? Are your friends? How did it affect you? How did it affect them? What kind of emotions did you experience, and what did you witness from your parents?
>
> Do you have any emotional reaction when you think about the prospect of a divorce? Your past experiences can affect the way you view this topic and your decision-making. Do you have a relationship with your father or mother despite the divorce? Are you the person preventing the development of a relationship with your estranged parent? Keep this in mind while reading.

When people are responding to something highly emotional, they can say and do things that they would never do otherwise. They can be blinded by feelings of anger, betrayal, disappointment, sadness, or whatever it may be. These are powerful feelings that can make people seek revenge or otherwise "get back at you" in any way possible. And when those emotions take over, they may not be willing to be reasonable.

Sure, some marriages end amicably, but many become emotional and sometimes contentious affairs. That prenup can keep the messy emotions out of the proceedings and protect your assets if your marriage ends. A prenup is the marriage equivalent to life insurance: you don't want to ever use it, but by preparing the document when things are good, you save yourself from the worst-case scenario if your situation changes.

If your partner is adamantly against a prenuptial agreement, try to assuage their fears. Acknowledge that you're preparing for that possible route, but make sure you emphasize the practicality of a "divorce plan" and show your commitment to your marriage. This is a discussion worth having. Despite how uncomfortable it may be, you'll save yourself and your partner a lot of pain and money if you establish protective measures now.

Take it from me. Like most people, I never could have imagined that my marriage would have ended. When I made those vows, I expected them to really be forever. That turned out to not be the case. And because we had never discussed that possibility prior, the process was even more difficult and devastating than it ever had to be.

My ex-wife and I knew our marriage was over, but I thought that we had agreed to be supportive co-parents. The divorce proceedings shook our commitment to that. Her lawyers tried to paint me as a wealthy doctor who wasn't home enough to support our kids. In reality, I was sitting on a mountain of debt, having just finished medical school and moving into surgical residency training. I hadn't prepared for the end of my marriage and in the courtroom, even my medical license became a so-called asset in the court of law.

A divorce isn't just the end of a marriage. Every aspect of your life is on the line. Your assets and property are the most apparent "things" to be divided. Beyond that, you enter discussions on custody—should the parents get equal access to the kids, or will one parent be given primary custody? Child support payments are expected, even if you go into debt to hire a decent lawyer to represent you.

Beyond these months of pain and tension, you may also suffer parental alienation. It seems like an obvious cost of a divorce, but the long-term damage is severe. We've all heard stories of children siding with one parent. Even if your children seek to remain neutral, they often become the rope in an emotional game of tug-of-war between you and your ex. That's psychologically damaging for everyone involved and those injuries may never heal properly. A prenup won't repair the unavoidable emotions that come with a family separating, but it can create a practical plan for co-parenting should a divorce occur. Statistics show that a divorce occurs every 42 seconds in the US. With such a high frequency, it's best to be prepared.

Alimony is another cost of an ending marriage. Your partner can demand reparation or financial support both during the divorce proceedings, and after. A partner who earns $50k a year could pay as much as $10k in alimony. Oftentimes, the alimony is so high that your average person can't pay it in one payment.

You may be thinking that you're not able to protect yourself well in case your marriage ends in divorce. Knowing the possible scenarios and how to prevent them is an easy way to start protecting yourself. There's the old saying: "Hope for the best but prepare for the worst." Prenuptials and asset protection are the embodiment of that, and as you've seen, it's worth the conversation. If you were running a marathon, you wouldn't jump in, sight unseen, and get moving. You would want to know the course: how many hills, the number of drink stations on the way, the weather, etc. It's the same with divorce. By being aware of the obstacles ahead of time, you can plan accordingly and won't be blindsided.

I experienced loss in my divorce that can't even be quantified. Sure, I paid money for an attorney and paid child support and more, but it's the unseen losses that make divorce proceedings so costly. My connection to my kids was damaged. Between the disrupted time with them and her attorneys using them as pawns, our relationships were tarnished. Losing access, time, and ultimately a connection with my children is the absolute worst outcome of the divorce. Nothing could ever make up for that.

Another cost was the time and energy that I could have been putting into my profession. Even during "inactive" times of the divorce when I was not in the courtroom or with attorneys, I was still thinking about it and not able to fully commit to my work, the way I wanted to. A less dedicated person could easily have had their entire career derailed by a divorce. For me, I was simply exhausted and wanted to give even more to medicine. For example, I did not have the time to add extra research projects. I considered a pediatric hand surgery fellowship in Australia, but divorce eliminated that goal. You can say to yourself that you won't bring personal baggage into the workplace, but you and I both know it's not that simple to wall up your emotions. The stress, fatigue, and uncertainty don't leave just because you've pulled into your parking space.

No, you're not one of the richest people in the world. But if you think it'll only take an hour to split up your assets and move on, you're in for a rude awakening. And that's why divorce coaching is a necessary investment. Reading books like this de-romanticizes the seemingly straightforward nature of divorce, even if it's an amicable one. Educate yourself on the process and you'll become less of a target for money-motivated attorneys. And if you're a high-value individual entering divorce proceedings, the stakes are even higher. Let's take a look at some real-life cases.

CHAPTER THREE
It Happened to Them, and It Could Happen to You

Many courthouses have a statue of Lady Justice just outside the entrance. She's a symbolic representation of the legal system, depicted as a woman holding balanced scales in one hand and a sword in the other. Most surprisingly, she is also always wearing a blindfold because, as they say, "Justice is blind." This means that the legal system is supposed to be an impartial and fair judge of any case that comes through. The outcome is ultimately only based on the truth and the law, and everything else is irrelevant. This is why it is called justice, after all—right?

Well, unfortunately, this isn't always how things work out. We have all seen how many judicial systems have ruled unfairly based on the facts of the people involved (race, gender, sexuality, wealth, etcetera) rather than the facts of the case. We even have a word for it—discrimination. While this has gotten better in recent years, it is still incredibly difficult for the supposed "justice" system to remain objective, especially when certain types of people and factors are involved.

So that said, not all divorces are going to be treated the same. What should be a simple process has been turned into an incredibly profitable industry (that is, for the attorneys and one ex-partner), so high-value individuals are especially targeted here. And when there's money on the table, the typical ethics and codes of conduct are tossed out the window by exes, attorneys, and judges alike. And because they think you have more to take, you have more to lose than the average person. The only way for you to "win" is simply to avoid the game altogether.

Just to be clear, we are only ever referring to cases without any criminal element involved. When someone is abusive to their spouse or neglective to their kids, that is a whole different situation. I have no sympathy for anyone like that, much less advice, so please keep that in mind. In this book, we are only talking about a divorce where the individual in question has not committed any sort of offense.

Even when a high-value individual hasn't done anything wrong, they have a "mark" against them, and it's simply that they have something that the attorneys and ex stand to gain. High-value individuals will be unfairly targeted in a divorce even in the best of cases.

When it comes to swaying the courts in their favor and making you pay, attorneys and exes have a number of dirty tricks up their sleeve. One of the easiest tactics is for an ex, especially if they are female, to simply say, "I feel unsafe." These three vague words can often be enough for a judge to grant a restraining order, even if there's no actual proof or even any accusations that you have done something to warrant one. The only reason they do this is to create fake evidence for their attorneys to paint a nasty picture in court later on.

While they may not explicitly say that you are in some way abusive or threatening (that would be perjury), the restraining order will loudly do that for them. It puts the burden on yourself to prove innocence. We all know that's not how it's supposed to work—everyone is supposedly innocent before proven guilty.

Then again, it's your word against a restraining order, so who do you think a judge is going to believe? Attorneys are experts at playing these technically-legal cards, and they do it all of the time.

However, they won't just operate in the legal gray zone. In fact, attorneys and exes will take it a step further and make false accusations of abuse outright. Again, it can be very difficult to disprove these accusations. It's your word versus theirs, and they may fabricate corroborative evidence to back up their claims. This is a tragically common scenario that many people have fallen victim to at great expense.

When the sharks smell blood in the water, nothing is left sacred. Even children have been used like pawns to gain the upper hand in court. At best, they'll just be encouraged to say things like they don't want to spend time with one parent, and they prefer the other one. But it's not unheard of for children to be coached to make allegations of horrific and untrue nature against their own father or mother. The child and parent can be torn apart and traumatized forever, and for what? Money? It is downright disgusting what people will do to get another dime, but we all have to understand that is the reality of things.

This isn't to say that this will definitely happen in a divorce case. If caught, the offending ex stands to lose everything, so the most egregious and illegal tactics are only used in a small percentage of cases. Oftentimes, they don't even really "need" to do these things, anyways. Many high-value individuals with a seemingly straightforward case will get financially suckerpunched just for making more than their ex. Being successful and having wealth is all it takes for a judge to decide to give it to your ex. But don't just take it from me—let's discuss some famous real-life cases of high-value individuals suffering financially because of a divorce.

One real-life case involves a former WWE wrestler who played a gaudy character with an ultra-rich lifestyle to match. Well, that portrayal seems a lot more like fiction than real life after multiple failed marriages. He has been ordered to pay his most recent ex-wife $4,000 in alimony every single month, an amount he was not able to afford. A warrant in Texas was once issued for his arrest over unpaid alimony. Allegedly, he owed $32,352.51, an amount that roughly equated to about eight months. He explained that he was unable to pay in that time because the tragic death of his son and his own health issues prevented him from working, but the courts had no sympathy. He is currently still working as a senior, likely to be able to keep signing these checks.

Another example involves a world-class heavyweight boxer who has made hundreds of millions of dollars throughout his career. He has also been married to and had children with several women, which has racked up multiple alimony and child support payments to his monthly bills over the years. One ex-wife was even able to successfully argue for an increase in the payment amount, which happens all the time and could even happen to you (more on that later). All of this has clearly led to some financial strain, and his home ended up foreclosing during a divorce in 2010. He is still working and, unsurprisingly, still making the news for new alimony and child support disputes.

One former NFL star who has had several children with several different women reportedly pays almost $45,000 every single month in child support. While that may have been affordable during the peak of his career, he's most likely not making that kind of money anymore. His failure to pay on time and disputes with his co-parents has resulted in a dramatic episode on a talk show and several threats of arrest for falling behind on payments.

All of these individuals have enjoyed long and successful careers, and yet all of these individuals have been financially crippled by the courts. And because they are famous, these supposedly private struggles are *very* public. News about their "baby mama drama" and divorce disputes often trump news about their accomplishments. The media lambasts every detail of these petty theatrics, which certainly can't help their reputations and careers.

The worst thing about many of these cases is that it could have been prevented. If high-value individuals like yourself understood what could possibly happen in a divorce, you may think twice about marrying without any protection. In the next few chapters, we will be going through all of the different components and potential outcomes that a divorce may have. By taking the time to understand and consider these things, you can also take the first steps to prevention.

CHAPTER FOUR

Settlements and Asset Loss

Almost all cases of divorce are going to include some kind of settlement. Similar to a lawsuit, a settlement is essentially an agreement to end the divorce process. Although the word might have some negative legalese type of connotations, a settlement is not necessarily a bad thing. A settlement is often the way for both parties to finalize the terms of their divorce and move on with their lives.

Settlements usually include two components: pay and time. Pay can mean the one-and-done check that one person will have to write another, or the monthly payments that need to be made going forward. If children are involved, time means determining the division of custody between the two parents.

If both partners are looking to end things amicably and/or build a healthy co-parenting relationship, then a settlement is helpful for doing so. In those cases, I always recommend working out the terms of the settlement together *without the legal system*. Ideally, the only time that an attorney should get involved is to officially write up the documents and finalize the divorce. Even when both parties are on the same page, the courts and attorneys are only looking to complicate the process in order to profit.

There should not exist a so-called "divorce industry" in America. And there definitely should not be any reason whatsoever why that divorce industry is worth approximately $28 billion *per year*. The wedding industry, where people are actually paying for legitimate goods and services to conduct an important ceremony, is not worth nearly that much. A "marriage industry" of actually filing the legal paperwork does not even exist.

It takes a couple of papers to enter into a marriage. In theory, it also only takes a couple of papers to leave one. So why is it almost always more complicated than that? Think about it: there are entire law practices dedicated to divorce. Attorneys wouldn't specialize in divorce proceedings if they haven't figured out how to extract as much money from the situation as they can.

If you and your ex can communicate with each other to figure out the terms of finalizing the divorce, then getting the courts involved will needlessly draw things out at a high cost. Two people who are focused on making the situation fair have a much better chance of actually doing so than any court ever could. If possible, always try to come to an agreement and bring in an attorney only when you are both ready to sign.

Training for Game Day

If you have not yet gotten married, I strongly recommend you consider signing a prenup. A prenup is like an alternative game plan that you draw up with your partner to prepare for the worst-case scenario. By having a prenup in place, you already have an agreement to turn to if the relationship doesn't work out.

When this cannot happen, then the terms of the settlement will be determined by the courts. During my divorce, I believed that everything would be based on straightforward calculations.

If the purpose of a settlement is to be fair to all parties, then I thought that the courts would simply look at each of our incomes and go from there. To me, things seemed pretty simple. They could just base everything off of those numbers, right?

Well, no. As it turns out, these apparent "calculations" get a lot less straightforward the more money that you (may or may not) have. While this system was originally designed to help protect women who were dependent on their spouse's income and could not earn money for themselves, the system has not been modified since that time to account for the growing equality between the sexes. Many people have taken advantage of the outdated system in order to extract as much from their ex as possible.

Attorneys are experts at influencing the courts in their client's favor. As we've just talked about, one thing they do when the divorce papers are served is to file a restraining order against their client's ex. The restraining order is oftentimes completely baseless and the attorney knows that, so they instruct their client to give a vague reason like "I feel unsafe." The burden of proof falls on the other to show that nothing happened, and their character is tarnished in front of the court.

That kind of misrepresentation is critical to exploitation, but attorneys will also often use the children as pawns to win their case. They will claim that their client's ex is an "unfit parent" in order to push for primary custody. If the ex can take primary custody, then they can also argue for more child support. Every tactic points back to their ultimate goal: to make you pay.

The payout in a settlement depends on many factors, including those aforementioned outside influences. A court will supposedly look at each respective income and the joint assets. In the fairest situation, only the assets acquired during the marriage would be split evenly between the two. If one person makes substantially more, then they may have to pay their ex child support in order to support an "equal lifestyle" between the two households. At least, that's how it should be.

It is rarely ever like this in practice. Like I've said, the system is constantly taken advantage of by people looking to "double dip", or collect in the settlement *and* work. When the ex is looking only to increase their cash flow, you are in for a rough time.

Assets are not just defined as bank accounts, cars, and properties. They can also go after your retirement, 401k, even your insurance policy. All of these (and more) are considered assets and, therefore, up for grabs in the court of law.

What is considered an asset can vary based on state laws. I've learned this the hard way. I was once married in the state of New York. Neither my ex or I ever *lived* there together, just married. When we ended up getting divorced, we had to go through the New York court system and their laws. This ended up greatly affecting the outcome of the settlement.

At the time, New York had a law that counted a medical license as equal to a piece of property. With property, the law requires either one of two things. If they sell the property, then they have to split the proceeds, despite the fact that she had property (a penthouse in Manhattan). Why would a New York court consider a medical license property as if it were owned by both individuals? Divorce is a billion-dollar industry. The laws and divorce process at times feel criminal. If they can get money out of you, they will—despite how hard you work for your money.

The court decided that I would have to pay my ex based on the apparent worth of my medical degree. They quantified this payout by taking an average surgeon's salary (even though I was not yet even making that) and multiplied it by a certain number of years. Somehow, that came to one million dollars.

Despite never making nearly that much, I was ordered to give my ex 33% of that. She herself had an MBA and made a separate income, but that did not seem to matter. Her degree was not considered property, just mine. We were two educated people who made our own money and never actually even lived together. It made no sense that one had to pay the other.

I guess it didn't make much sense to the state of New York either, because they later took that law off of the books. You'd think that helped in my case, but you'd be mistaken. People are not freed from jail when their crime is no longer illegal. The courts *don't* backtrack like that, even when they are wrong. That is just one of the reasons why you have to be so careful.

Courts never backtrack and it is very difficult to get them to reassess, and that can be particularly bad for athletes. Athletes often only make so much for so long. The "big money" years of their career are numbered like no other profession. If they happen to get a divorce during this time, the court will only look at those few years to judge what they have to pay. That number will almost never get readjusted when their income inevitably drops.

That even happened to me. I once went from a solid surgeon's salary to zero in the span of two weeks when I had to have unanticipated heart surgery. There was no forbearance, no nothing. Nobody cared. No matter what, I was still obligated to write that check. If I was even *late* to do so, I could have my license suspended or even go to jail. You can really get treated like an actual criminal over money.

Assets also aren't just monetary. Especially for high-value individuals, your time and energy are the priceless assets that you get robbed of during this process.

Let's just talk about the actual time you might lose to the actual divorce. Since bureaucratic processes are involved, it takes an astronomical amount of time to fill out paperwork, meet with attorneys, and go to hearings. This is all time that a high-value individual often does not have to begin with.

I certainly did not. Like any typical professional, I was working the weekday 9-5. Of course, this is also when all court hearings occur. They don't have any evening or weekend options. So, I had to take time off for each and every hearing.

That time must come from somewhere, and I realized at the end of the year where mine came from: my vacation. Those days all added up. I nickel-and-dimed all the PTO (Paid Time Off) I had, and then some. All of my vacation *and* personal days went into showing up to court and getting exploited for it. It was a very demoralizing thing to realize.

Not only did I have to spend my own vacation days on the hearings, but I also had to travel out of state for them. I did not live where we had gotten married. Because of state laws, there was no option to move hearings to where I was. It's all about the convenience of the courts, and that came at a huge cost to me.

These legal proceedings are not only time-consuming but can be exhausting. All of that time and traveling made it extremely difficult to focus on my actual career. My focus, energy, and peace of mind were challenged during all of this. My physical health even suffered. It took quite some time to recover.

Stop and Think

> If you have not experienced a divorce or that of your parents, you have almost certainly witnessed someone else go through a divorce. How did they appear to be doing throughout the process? Did their mental, physical, or emotional health seem to suffer? Did they have any new problems in their job or other relationships as a result of the divorce? Most likely, you've answered "yes" to most of these questions. Remember: if it can happen to them, it can happen to you. A divorce is an event that can affect all aspects of a person and their lives if they are not adequately prepared for it.

My career depends on my ability to flawlessly practice the skills that I have learned for decades. As a surgeon, there is no room for error. I had to work extra hard not to allow my ordeal to impact my work. It was a very, very difficult period that I just managed to get through.

The professional athlete has to maintain peak physical health in order to perform at their full capacity. Stress has a very real impact on health. When measured on the Holmes-Rahe stress scale, divorce is the second highest stressor, second to the death of a spouse. The stress of a divorce can have an effect on long-term health. A study found that those who were divorced or widowed were 20% more likely to develop chronic conditions such as heart disease, diabetes, or cancer. This can drastically affect performance, which could cause further issues in their life and career. An athlete quite often cannot afford to lose the time they need for training and to maintain their bodies. Without that necessary time and energy, they often cannot perform at the elite level. Out of the make-or-break things that can happen, a divorce could easily "break" their career just from the immaterial impact it has on their well-being.

Luckily, this kind of loss and stress is not some inevitable event. Loss can be greatly mitigated by having some forethought and being cautious throughout the process.

Firstly, a lot of this can be avoided by having a prenuptial agreement in place. A prenup will define all of the assets that each person came into the marriage with so that those assets are not divided during a divorce. It's especially important that a high-value individual has their partner agree to (and sign) a prenup because they often come into the marriage with numerous assets.

Beyond defining these "hands off" assets, a prenup can also set the terms of any potential divorce settlement. If you are even just considering having children, then I strongly recommend including some guidelines for a co-parenting relationship. At the very least, have that conversation with your partner. You don't want to find out that they plan to take full custody in the case of a divorce only after that situation occurs.

A prenup is a precaution that can happen only before marriage. Many are often well past that point by the time they seek out this advice. I've worked with a lot of people who retrospectively wish that they had gotten a prenup and spared themselves all of the ensuing issues. However, it's not the only thing that can be done.

Awareness and understanding is critical as well. You need to be aware of what is going on and do your due diligence to understand the laws of the state that you got married, divorced, and live in. Any and all variances could come to affect the terms of your settlement. A destination wedding in Central Park might mean that an odd state law specific to New York will come back to hurt you. By being aware of the legislation and how the courts make their determinations, you can better anticipate and prepare for what they might throw at you.

Training for Game Day

When writing a prenup and getting married, consider any and all applicable state laws and take them into account. Any state that you get married, lived, and get divorced in can factor into the outcome of your divorce. If you move or if the laws change, stay updated to understand how they may affect you in the case of a divorce.

Awareness also extends to being aware of what comes out of your mouth. Remember, attorneys are not your friend. You have to watch what you say to them. It's almost like interrogation. They are going to take anything and everything that you say and twist it to create leverage.

My initial naivete with this process hurt me here, too. I answer all questions honestly and openly. This is what I did when the attorneys asked me different questions, and it was all turned into ammo to drive up the price that I was going to pay.

For example, I was asked whether or not I would my children to go to private school. At the time, in my opinion, it depended on where we lived. If that particular district had good public schools, then they should go to the public school. If not, they should go to private school. This is exactly what I said.

Somehow, this became so that the kids had to go to the most expensive private school that my ex found, and *I* had to pay for it. Now that would have been fine by me if we had talked about it and I planned for it, but this was all just unexpectedly thrown into the settlement to add to the check that I had to write.

Treat any and all questions like they are going to be used against you and answer accordingly. Don't ever give them more than they need to know. You are not being "helpful" by providing that extra information, I promise.

For the high-value individual, they cannot actually give anything extra. Don't try to be generous with what you say or what you include in the settlement. That might sound harsh but understand that you can and will be held to anything that's in there. If you suddenly cannot pay what you originally could, that will be your problem and your problem alone.

A settlement can often mean taking a huge financial hit in order to finalize the divorce. You can lose money, property, valuables, and other assets, not to mention the priceless things like time and energy. But, this is just a one-time thing that many can eventually recover from.

That's supposing that you aren't obligated to any ongoing payments like alimony and child support. Writing these court-ordered checks every month can often be what brings a high-value individual from wealth to ruin. That's next.

CHAPTER FIVE

Alimony and Child Support

As we've already covered, a settlement is the way to end a divorce. That can include a lump-sum payout to the other party, but it could also mean making monthly alimony or child support payments. While a one-time payment can represent a huge hit to your bank account all at once, these continuous bills often incur way more damage to your personal finances over time. In some cases, you can even end up totally broke.

Alimony, also known as spousal support, is basically a court order to pay an ex spouse a certain amount of money. This could be either a single payout to finalize the divorce or as recurring payments over a period of time. Whether you will have to pay alimony and how much is supposedly determined by the income disparity between the two partners and any relevant financial factors, but it clearly gets a lot more complicated in the actual court system.

The purpose of alimony, at least as I understand it, is to equalize the way that one was living during the marriage. The partner that makes less has become accustomed to a certain lifestyle, and I suppose that alimony is meant to account for that. However, this reasoning doesn't exactly seem fair when you consider that would mean the other person has to continue providing financial support after their marriage has ended.

To me, it's like if you took a friend out to lunch every day. They may not have asked for it, but they certainly didn't object either. And you didn't mind it. Then one day, for whatever reason, you are no longer friends. But then your old friend still expects you to buy their lunch. Alimony is more or less the same thing. Neither makes any sense.

Alimony is another byproduct of a system that was built for a completely different time. Back when women were legally and socially barred from making the same level of income that men could, alimony was one thing that the system provided to ensure that they would not fall in poverty. Their systemic dependence on their husband was recognized, and that had to be accounted for in a divorce. In a society that did not give them the ability to really support themselves, alimony was fair.

Stop and Think

What kind of relationship do you and your partner have? Or, if you are single, what kind of relationship do you want? One where one person depends on the other, or a relationship of two equal partners supporting each other?

As times have progressed, most people prefer the latter. So why should the terms of the relationship change after it ends? If someone is capable of providing for themselves, does it make sense for their ex to do so instead?

But society has changed. While we have a ways to go in many respects, it definitely isn't the 50s anymore. Women are going to college and getting degrees *more* than men are. They have the education and the ability to make a near-equal, equal, or even more money than men. There is no longer the widespread social expectation for women to sacrifice their careers to stay at home and raise children, either. Nowadays, a woman does not have to be reliant on her spouse.

While our society has started to move toward equality, the courts do not yet recognize two people as equal. At this point, alimony is often nothing more than a relic of a very outdated system. In the case of my second marriage, she had an M.B.A. from an Ivy League university. I had gotten my medical license well beforehand. We had no children and had never even *lived together*. Yet, the laws and practices that were somehow still in place decided that I had to pay her over $300k to make our separation equitable. The attorneys she could afford to hire certainly helped with that, too.

Attorneys know that this system is antiquated and are the masters of exploiting it to the fullest extent. If they smell money, they are going to figure out a way to get it. They may look for any possible factors they could use to argue for more. Baseless allegations of abuse or infidelity are not uncommon here. Not that they even "need" these things for alimony to be granted. In most states, all the ex has to do is prove that you were the more successful spouse to tip the scales in their favor.

Real-World Examples

It's not just men. While men are most often ordered to pay up, successful women have also been affected by these laws as well. Karen McCullah is a very successful screenwriter in California. She's known for writing iconic films such as *Ten Things I Hate About You* and *Legally Blonde*. She also was reportedly ordered to pay her ex-husband $6,000 every month for years after their divorce due to alimony laws in her state. In a world where women are increasingly out-earning their male counterparts and partners, it's important to recognize that the laws originally designed to protect them are now negatively affecting them as well.

Because the system is simply not fair to the current society that we live in, it's really difficult to defend yourself against an alimony request. If they ask for it, they in all likelihood will get it. Having the money to hire a good lawyer can help mitigate the loss. If you can pay, then you can win, so long as you can also stick it out for the lengthy legal battle.

You also need to have the stamina to not be worn down to compliance. People rarely talk about just how tedious and draining the constant hearings and negotiations with the attorneys can be. I was in and out of the courts for ten years until

I signed an agreement for my second marriage. There were times where I was so exhausted that I would have been willing to sign *anything* just to get out of there.

The divorce process can often work the way that some unethical interrogations do. If you've ever seen those shows on false confessions, then you know how it goes: crooked cops will keep someone in a little room for hours on end and repeatedly lie to confuse and manipulate the "suspect." They get them to the point that they will confess to whatever they tell them to just in the hope of going home. It's an extreme analogy, but that's *exactly* what it feels like, albeit on a much smaller scale.

Like a lot of other things, the best way to prevent this is with a prenup. A prenup can stipulate that neither person is able to request or receive alimony in the case of a divorce. By making this stipulation go both ways, a potential spouse can see that it covers them as well and be more likely to sign it.

For a young couple who may only be at the start of their careers, an alimony clause in their prenup could come to protect either or both of them. They never know who will end up making more money. For a high-value individual, an alimony clause in their prenup is just smart. If you enter the marriage as the higher earner already, then it will be very difficult later on to get out of alimony payments. And if your partner seriously objects to an alimony clause, then that could possibly hint at their true intentions.

A prenup can sometimes be all that you need to protect yourself from alimony requests, but it cannot remove the possibility of paying child support. And it shouldn't; after all, child support is intended to ensure your child's quality of life. Any parent should be happy to pay that. Here, it's a matter of making sure it is an appropriate amount and used for its intended purposes.

The purpose of child support is to support an equal lifestyle in each household and make sure that all of their needs are met: housing, food, healthcare, clothing, school supplies, etcetera. If you have a child and make more money than your ex, expect to write a check each month until your youngest turns eighteen. That's just how it is.

Again, that's how it should be. Living between two homes is already a difficult situation for your children to face. Child support, especially in a coparenting relationship, can often help at least remove any additional issues in their lives. But like everything else in the divorce industry, even this unquestionably fair aspect will get used as a money-grabbing tactic.

If there are two loving and capable parents, then custody will ideally be split an even 50/50 and the child support is assessed based on that divide. Child support increases correlatively with physical custody. The more you have your kids, the less you will usually have to pay your ex. So if one person is looking to exploit the other, then they will often fight for full custody in order to bump up the checks.

In all the nastiness of the divorce industry, this is where it gets the ugliest. Parents and attorneys alike will use innocent children as pawns in their game with no regard for what that could do to them. A traumatic divorce and custody battle can seriously affect a child's emotional development. Parental alienation is a particularly devastating possibility that can happen here, which we will talk about in Chapter Five.

If nothing criminal has happened and no abuse has occurred, child support is almost always the unspoken incentive for going after full custody. Custody battles are downright awful for everyone and I always advise staying as far away from the courts as possible, especially here. The best thing to do is to prevent it from even happening by establishing a co parenting relationship with your ex.

Co parenting is key, especially for professional athletes. If you have a fluctuating schedule and are constantly on the road for games, then a co parenting relationship will allow you to have more flexible custody. A co parent is more likely to let you have the kids during your summers off than a hostile ex. As co parents, you can work out finances and time with the kids together rather than abiding by what's strictly on paper. We'll talk more about how to establish and maintain a healthy co parenting relationship after a divorce or separation in Chapter Six.

Stop and Think

If you are a child of divorce, can you remember how your family's dynamic changed? Was it a smooth transition, or a difficult one? How did it affect you? Can you say whether your parents were co parents or hostile toward each other?

As a high-value target, you have to be aware that having children with someone that you are not married to will have some of the same legal ramifications as getting married. Creating another human life with someone can tie you to that person a lot like an actual contract can. More so, even; you will have to maintain contact with that other parent in some way for the rest of your life. Deciding *who* to have children with is just as important as having children at all. Marriage is not always for forever, but parenthood definitely is.

Sometimes, children may come as an unexpected blessing in your life. There have been more than a few professional athletes who have had unplanned children. Frankly, the frequent traveling and starstruck fans can lead to some…well, let's just say some ill-advised encounters. The only reason we are even talking about this is because there have been many publicized instances of someone attempting to "baby trap" an athlete or other high-value individual by getting pregnant specifically to claim child support. This happens especially to athletes due to their fame and vulnerability of being young, usually naive, and constantly on-the-go.

Real-World Examples

This really happens. One Instagram influencer and fitness model, who has been known to make social media posts alluding to her intent to seduce younger professional athletes, has been accused of "baby-trapping" an NBA player. The NBA player was 22 and she was 28 when she became pregnant with his child and have since separated. While she went on a podcast to defend herself and made the solid point that he was equally responsible for their child's conception, allegations remain that she had sought out the younger and perhaps naive young man with the intention of getting child support.

And it happens so often, high-value men often take (odd) precautions. In 2022, an Instagram model alleged that a popular musician admitted to pouring hot sauce in a condom before discarding it after their sexual encounter. She found this out after taking it from the bathroom trash and attempting to impregnate herself, only to experience a severe burning sensation. The musician has not made any official comments on her claims, but did post a cryptic response on Instagram that seemingly confirmed the incident did occur.

However, this is not to say that getting "baby trapped" is common either. It's just another one of those things that a high-value target needs to be aware of and watch out for. These days, most people having children outside of marriage have either decided to live as common-law spouses (i.e. partners who are not legally married) or had an accidental pregnancy.

If you have a child outside of marriage and are no longer living with or in a relationship with the other parent, then there are a few critical things to consider. Especially as a father not married to the mother, you may not necessarily have the same automatic legal rights to your child as a married father would. The most important matter in that situation comes right after your child is born: the birth certificate.

Getting your name on the birth certificate will legally establish you as the father of your child and it will help you build a much better "case" should you have to fight for your custody rights. Conversely, signing your name on the birth certificate and legally establishing yourself as the father will nearly guarantee child support. Which obviously shouldn't be an issue in most cases, but this can prove problematic if the child turns out to not biologically be yours.

Yes, this happens. If you sign the birth certificate, you have claimed paternity of that child and any related legal responsibilities. It will take a lengthy court battle to "reverse" that if needed. There are even cases where a man has still been compelled to pay child support for a child that they did not biologically father because they had signed the birth certificate.

Even with a DNA test to prove it, courts will sometimes uphold the child support order simply because of the name on the paper.

> ### Real-World Examples
>
> **It's not just those with money.** In 2019, a man in Florida was ordered by the courts to continue paying more than a third of his paychecks to support a child that was not his. He had signed the original birth certificate, but a paternity test soon proved that he was not the biological father, a devastating blow further compounded by the fact that he was still "on the hook" for child support. The mother of the child even appealed to the courts to discontinue the payments, but they argued that he was the legal father and thus responsible. The man could not afford an attorney to appeal the decision, so he has been forced to represent himself—and continue paying in the meantime.

Again this is not necessarily a *likely* scenario, but just one of the many things that a high-value target has to consider. If there is any actual question, it is smart to get a paternity test and know for sure before putting your name on anything.

Whether you have children in a marriage, a relationship, or at all, you are almost guaranteed to pay some amount of child support if you are no longer with the other parent. If the relationship with that other parent has become hostile and exploitative, then it can honestly feel pretty bad to write those checks every month, especially if you don't get to even see your children. Let's talk a bit about how to avoid one of those worst-case scenarios.

Like I've already said, you can do yourself a huge favor just by educating yourself on how the industry works and the specifics of your situation. Study up on any and all state laws that could apply to you: this could mean the state you live in, got married, got divorced, where the kids live, where anybody may be moving to, etcetera. While some places have been more active in updating the laws on their books to keep up with the times, others are still dragging their feet. The Southern region as a whole seems to be most notably archaic regarding child support and custody.

By knowing how the court system works, you'll also see for yourself just how important it is not to offer anything "extra" or otherwise allow them to affix you to more than the minimum of what you can afford. I personally understand how you may want to "prove" to the attorneys just how dedicated you are to your children by verbalizing what you are willing to provide for them and being upfront to their questions. All this really does is put you on the hook in a way that can really hurt you later on.

I'm not saying to only pay the bare minimum support for your children; just to have only the minimum on the books. Of course you are happy to pay whatever you need to help your children, but you may not always be able to pay *everything* all of the time.

Anybody's life and circumstances can change at the drop of a hat. If you suddenly find yourself facing a hardship, you are not going to find any sympathy with the courts. When I had open-heart surgery and could not work, I was told to either pay up or lose my license. Nobody would even consider a temporary grace period on my payments. Whatever you are ordered to pay is what you have to pay, no matter what.

Technically that amount *can* change, but it's almost never going to be in your favor. You can always request a reassessment based on a change in income. However, it isn't immediate; it's a process like anything else and you're going to have to write a check to get through it. You still need to pay for an attorney, fill out paperwork, provide all of the right documents, and deal with the courts. It's going to take a lot of time and money for them to even consider it.

At one point in my career, I tried to go back to the courts for a reassessment. I had been receiving a captain's salary as a military doctor (medical license or not, you get paid the same as anyone in your rank) while supplementing my income by working in clinics on the side. After I got out of the military, I went back to surgical training to finish my specialty. I was now making about half as much as I used to, so I really couldn't afford to pay what the court had ordered.

Now, I was only asking for lower payments for the four years that it took to finish my training. I'd be making a much higher salary as a specialist after that and was happy to pay more as a result. My request seemed pretty reasonable with everything considered.

I wrote the check, jumped the hoops, and went through the whole reassessment process just to hear the court say,

"Nope." They decided that because I already had my medical license and didn't "need" to finish my specialty, my income drop would somehow be self-imposed and therefore not worth a reassessment. Mind you, I had put it out there that *I would eventually make a lot more money*. This temporary reduction was so that I could make more, and pay more, in the long run. But they didn't want to hear it.

They weren't willing to adjust for my lower income when I requested it. Yet, they are *always* willing to adjust when you're making more. If they think that you're getting any more money, they want to put that in their own pocket. That's how it is.

For high-value individuals, your income can't always be counted on exactly every month. It can fluctuate substantially. And for the pro athlete, your income is eventually going to drop. The unfortunate truth about an athletic career is that it has a sooner end date than others. You have to consider how you will make the transition out at some point and owing an "athlete's" amount of child support every month is going to kill your financial future.

A reassessment may prove to be a more worthwhile use of time, energy, and finances for a pro athlete after retiring from the field or court. It could be easier to prove that your income has dropped due to external circumstances, but you are still going to need to afford a good lawyer and be willing to go through the process. Still, successful reassessments are usually rare.

A reassessment also goes both ways. If the other parent thinks that you are now making more money than you did when the courts first calculated, they can go and apply for a reassessment every two years. This means that you will have to go through the process of hiring an attorney and revealing personal financial information to defend yourself.

If you really are making more, then you should definitely expect to pay more. That is unfortunately how it goes. But, a reassessment can backfire for them if it turns out that you are actually making less than you originally were. The best way to avoid a reassessment is to be discreet and not disclose any financial information to your ex that you do not have to tell them. In these dynamics, sharing information will only come to hurt you.

The absolute best way to avoid *all* of this is to have that co parenting relationship. In an ideal arrangement, you and the other parent can keep as much off the books as possible and work out an agreement that's best for both of you. An understanding co parent is going to readjust the custody where a hostile ex will not. And instead of writing one big check every month that you can't be sure will go toward your kids, you can pay for specific things: tuition, mortgage, grocery store gift cards, etcetera. You'll feel a lot better about spending that money and will probably end up spending even more money than the court would have ordered, and happily so.

Everyone wins in a co parenting relationship. This is really the absolute best case scenario in a divorce. Your best chance at establishing a co parenting relationship is to talk about it before you even get married or have kids. Co parenting, custody, and child support guidelines should be thoroughly discussed before marriage and even included in the prenup if possible.

Training for Game Day

Yes, you *can* include a co parenting agreement in a prenup! The following points should be discussed with your partner and included in the prenup:

- Basic custody division.
- Where "homebase," or the city where the children will be raised in, is.
- Religious or cultural aspects that each parent agrees to observe in both homes.
- Anything else that is important to you and your partner.

If kids are in the realm of possibility whatsoever, you and your partner need to take the responsibility to have that conversation, even if it may be uncomfortable. Talking about these things before kids are actually in the picture will give you a chance to establish an objective basis of how and what you will do if the marriage doesn't work out. It will also let you know what your partner would honestly have in mind if that were to happen.

Considering the possibility of a custody split is often worse than considering the possibility of a divorce. In a childless marriage, divorce normally only affects the two people. When kids are involved, it gets a lot more complicated. Both parents have to put aside their personal feelings about the other and the sadness of not always physically having your kids to become co parents. If you become a parent, you have to understand and accept that responsibility if the time comes. It's ultimately all for the wellbeing of the children.

Establishing the guidelines for a co parenting relationship as part of your prenup can also help avoid one of the worst things that can happen to any parent or child: loss of custody and parental alienation. This is no less than a tragedy compounded by the fact that it's almost always preventable. In cases where it is not, we will then discuss how to mitigate its damage.

CHAPTER SIX
Loss of Custody and Parental Alienation

We've already covered how custody will correlate to child support. While almost everyone will deny it, going for full custody is the common, unspoken tactic to getting more child support. But it's not always about the money; sometimes, it's about power. In an especially contentious divorce, one parent may try to get full custody simply to assert themselves over the other.

No matter the reason behind it, high-value individuals are automatically on the defense here. As they have time-intensive and demanding careers, they will often be forced to "prove" their ability to parent. Many courts will assume (and the ex's attorney will argue) that someone so dedicated to their profession can't also be dedicated to their children. While it's more than possible to manage a work and family life, high-value individuals typically have less time for all the court appearances and attorney meetings to disprove this accusation, which further complicates the matter. High-value individuals need to be prepared to prove they are capable of doing both by sacrificing time and providing the evidence.

Especially in the United States, men are typically at a disadvantage in custody battles. There are so many possible explanations for why there exists this bias against men (specifically in this regard), but the most likely may be due to the antiquated court system still in place. Similar to the outdated alimony laws, many courts favor mothers because women were the primary caregivers "back in the day," while men were the primary breadwinners. In the past patriarchal society, it wouldn't make sense to give more custody to the parent with the least time to care for the children.

Again, the world has changed quite a bit. Women are in the workforce just as much as men, and it has even become socially acceptable for the roles to reverse: there are an increasing number of "house husbands," or men who have elected to stay at home with young children while the mother works. For the courts to still assume that a woman is the primary caregiver is honestly sexist in this day and age.

Stop and Think

Oftentimes when a pro athlete gets to speak on camera, they'll say "Hi, Mom." How often do you hear them say, "Hi, Dad."? While it's a seemingly innocuous detail, this snub could show that many of these athletes do not have a relationship with their fathers. Why do you think that is?

Like many other people, their parents may have divorced. In this scenario, their mother was likely awarded primary custody. Did all of their fathers abandon them, or is there something else going on?

Still, if custody is not split equally, the mother is much more likely to be awarded primary custody. This is also likelier when the children are younger, especially elementary-age and under. For high-individuals who also happen to be men, you may be walking into the courtroom with two strikes already against you.

Without a healthy co parenting relationship, the best-case scenario is a cookie-cutter custody division that won't take other factors into account. You may get Monday through Thursday every week, but what if your mother's birthday falls on a Friday? What if you have a work trip during the week but want to take the kids for a 3-day weekend? If your co parent isn't willing to work with you on those varying occasions and the court has already ruled what days that you do and don't get, then you won't find any flexibility.

Flexibility in the schedule can prove immensely valuable for a high-value individual. For those with varying "work days" and who need to travel, like professional athletes, it can even be necessary. You can't take your kids on the road with you. Without that flexibility, some may be forced to choose their children over their career.

Custody equals control, too. The parent with the most custody, also called "parenting time," will not only receive more child support, but they will ultimately get to make more decisions. You get very little say when you have less custody. If they decide that your children should go to a certain private school, then they're going to that school (and you'll be paying the tuition). Your influence as a parent is greatly diminished when you do not get time with your children.

Time is ultimately what you have to fight for here, specifically overnights. The courts determine custody based on the nights that your child actually sleeps over. So, if they are at your house every single day but only sleep there on the weekends, then the other parent will still technically have primary custody.

Overnights versus day-only is one of the tactics the opposing attorney may use to mislead you into thinking you have more custody than you actually do. For example, if they offer you every other weekend and Wednesdays from 5:00pm-9:00pm, this may seem like a good deal. In reality, that time on Wednesday isn't counted and every other weekend is only 52 days out of the *entire year*. The court will divide those 52 overnights by 365 days and calculate a custody division of 86/14. And if your ex technically has the kids 86% of the time, the child support is going to reflect that.

While custody and child support are clearly tied together, you can never actually verbalize that at any point. It's the truth, but they'll crush you if you ever try to say it in court. More time awarded means less money paid, which makes it almost impossible to get more custody after the first decision is made. To avoid being misled into an unfair agreement in the first place, do the math and fight for your 50/50 upfront.

That 50/50 has to reflect equal overnights, since those are what the courts really count. Even if you pick your kids up from school every single day and attend all their soccer practices, the only thing taken into consideration is the number of nights they sleep at your house. That's it.

Make sure you adequately prepare to have your kids for half the time as well. It's not easy to argue for 50/50 if your kids don't have their own bedrooms set up at your house. You want your child to feel as "at home" with you as they are at the other parent's house. If you are truly trying to co-parent, then you have to have equal access and an equal home, too.

Training for Game Day

As co parents, it's important to ensure both houses have the same amenities and necessities as the other so nothing can be used as leverage. If your ex tries to keep them at their house because they bought them an Xbox, then you may want to consider getting them an Xbox, too. Ask your kids what they need in their new room and encourage them to decorate and take ownership of the space. Soon enough, they'll start to view both houses as their two "homes."

Equal access doesn't just mean equal overnights. You need to make sure you are on the contact list for every school, doctor, daycare, extracurricular program, anything your child is involved in. If another parent wants to assert control, they will often do this by blocking your ability to get critical information and make decisions for your children in these facilities. Equal access needs to be included in the custody agreement to make sure it is honored.

Nobody can deny how big of an adjustment this will be in you and your family's life. Even in the most amicable co-parenting situations, your children will need some time to get used to living in two homes. There is no getting around that.

With that said, you cannot let your ex try to tell you that 50/50 custody will be too disruptive for your childrens' lives or otherwise not in their best interest. Unfortunately, everyone's lives have already been disrupted by the divorce. Split custody is not going to somehow "hurt" your children any further. However, they will be harmed by losing out on a relationship with you. Like the other approximate 50% of children in the US whose parents have divorced, they will eventually adapt to this new way of life and thrive. If your ex suggests anything otherwise, it's most likely only a guilting tactic.

You are not the only person at risk of being manipulated. The children are the most vulnerable targets for being used in this way. It's so common, there's even a term for it: parental alienation.

"Parental alienation" at its baseline can be defined as the process by which one parent allows and encourages a child's rejection of the other parent. By manipulating the child to spurn a relationship with the other parent, they can then gain full custody and complete control. Parental alienation is much more common than many realize and has far-reaching effects on everyone involved.

Parental alienation should not be confused with "parental alienation syndrome" (PAS). Parental alienation syndrome was a hypothesized disorder specifically manifested in the child. It has been discredited since its introduction in the 1980s. PAS is not recognized by any accredited scientific organizations, such as the American Psychiatric Association, and is not found in the Diagnostic and Statistical Manual of Mental Disorders (DSM).

Parental alienation, however, can be classified as a form of "child psychological abuse," under guidelines in the most recent edition of the DSM. Induced parental alienation, if left untreated, can result in severe traumatic psychological and physical effects in the abused child.

This manipulation can come in a variety of ways. Sometimes, parental alienation may be obvious. One parent could divulge inappropriate details about the divorce to the children, tell lies about the other parent, or speak in a clearly disparaging manner about the other parent. Parental alienation could also become criminal in nature; as previously covered, there have been an unfortunate number of cases where one parent will coach a child to falsely accuse the other parent of abuse to secure custody.

These cases of parental alienation can often be more easy to spot and call out to the courts. In proven cases of parental alienation, it can backfire on the offending parent and they can end up losing custody or face other legal consequences. However, the more common form of parental alienation is so covert that you may not realize it's happening.

That's exactly what happened to me. Everything my ex did was so subtle that I constantly questioned whether or not it was even going on. This is how it is for many people. It's a lot like gaslighting. Nothing bad was ever overtly said, but the result is the same: losing a relationship with your kids.

It's difficult to pinpoint exactly *what* this covert alienation looks like. It can look different for everyone, but these are just a couple personal examples of what went on starting when my sons were two and eight all the way through their high school graduations.

Over the course of those sixteen or so years, there were *so* many times where I came to visit and they just weren't there. My ex would let me tell them, "Hey, I can't wait to see you!" I'd show up, they weren't there, but she would tell them, "I don't know why he didn't show up." Somehow, somewhere, the when-and-where of my visit would get muddled and I would miss them, but she'd let the kids think I didn't come at all. This slowly built up their distrust of me.

I only knew this was going on because of one particular birthday party that I had supposedly not bothered to come to. I had asked my ex if there were any plans for my son's birthday and never got an answer. Come to find out, there was actually a full-blown party I was not told about.

One of the people that attended the party was someone I knew. They later told me when other people asked where I was, my ex responded, "Oh, I don't know why he didn't come." Of course, she omitted the fact that *I did not know* this party was even happening. To everyone and my sons, it just looked like I didn't care.

There were so many instances where I was made out to be some kind of "deadbeat dad," some where I couldn't quite put my finger on *how* it was being done. There were times where I'd walk into their school and there was just this palpable negative energy around me. People were acting like I'd just spent 20 years in jail or something. I can only wonder what had been previously said or insinuated to make their teachers look and talk to me the way they did.

This happened more blatantly in court. Just to settle for one week with my kids out of their entire summer break, I had to send pictures of my house, license plate, and ID. It was never directly said, but they were treating me like I had done something in the past to warrant these kinds of precautions.

Negative energy is the unspoken side of parental alienation. Kids are really good at picking up on this stuff, and it makes everything that much worse. When I did get that week with my sons, they didn't seem too excited to see me. My youngest didn't want to be with me *at all*. I think my ex contributed greatly to that. Every time he spoke with her, he'd always end up crying when he got off the phone. I'd overhear her say things like:

> "I miss you so much.
> I just can't wait for you to come *home*."
>
> "Honey, your dog misses you so much!"
>
> "It's just not the same without you two here.
> We can't wait for you to come back."

Something about the tone of voice or how she phrased things, but she had a way of making him so upset every time she called. It got to the point where I asked the courts if they could keep her from calling so frequently and upsetting him like that. Of course, there was no way of stopping it.

It's natural for a child to miss their parent, but it shouldn't detract from their time with other one. A co-parent is critical to facilitating a good time with the other parent. My ex did nothing to support the kids having a good time with me. If anything, she was actively working against me. The energy wasn't, "Hey, go have a good time with your dad!" but, "You have to go with your dad."

She'd also guilt them for "having" to go, too. This tactic is pretty common: the ex will tell the kids that they don't like being alone in the house, they don't feel well, how sad they are without them, anything to make the kids feel guilty for going over to your house.

It puts you in a really horrible position. Instead of having quality time together, your kids are focused on missing the other parent and feeling bad for not being with them. They are upset and "homesick," and you become the bad guy for supposedly taking them away. It gets to be where you'd almost rather not see your kids at all so they don't have to go through that.

When I brought them back to my ex's house at the end of the week, she threw them a massive "Welcome Home" party. I dropped them off and saw all her friends and family come running out to hug them. You would have thought they had been gone for years, that's how over-the-top it was. But what really shocked me was the way everyone checked them over and asked, "Are you boys okay?", as though something had been *done* to them. That just blew me away.

The thing that's so horrible about this kind of alienation is not only do you question if it's happening, but it's almost impossible to explain what's going on to someone else. It's an indescribably painful and lonely thing to go through.

The kids might never understand that it happened, either. As a matter of fact, to this day, I am sure that they will deny it while being upset that I shared this information. They can look people straight in the eye and honestly say, "My mom/dad never said a bad word about them, but we just don't have a relationship." This is why covert alienation can be the most damaging form there is; if your child can't point to anything your ex ever explicitly said or did, then they will assume you were the problem all along.

> ### Stop and Think
>
> It's important for all children of divorce or separation to spend individual time with both of their parents and form their own opinions. If you don't have a relationship with one of your parents, think about why that may be. Was it something they did? Was it something said about them? Even as an adult reading this, it may be a good idea to give them a call and see for yourself.

It's really difficult to confront and stop parental alienation as it's happening, especially the more subtle tactics. With covert alienation, the offending parent sometimes may not even realize they are doing it. One of the best ways to prevent parental alienation before it occurs is to establish and actively maintain a healthy co-parenting relationship with your ex. Parental alienation is a lot less likely to occur when both of you are working together and supporting your respective times with the kids.

That said, the absolute best way to prevent all of this, again, is to get 50/50 custody upfront. Having time with your kids (independent from your ex's influence) is critical to developing a relationship with them. While your ex may still try to assert control and create negative energy around you, they won't be able to do as much when your kids are with you half the time.

As a high-value individual, the courts are automatically going to assume you are less involved with your children as your ex. They are not going to believe otherwise unless you have the documented evidence to prove it. This is why you should start recording the time and money you spend on your kids to show what you physically and financially "do" for them before you ever need evidence.

This doesn't have to be anything tedious; writing down when you go to your kid's practices on a calendar and keeping receipts of the summer camp you paid for will be enough. General documentation should be a part of a high-value individual's routine, anyways. It's these little things nobody pays attention to in the moment that suddenly become so important later on. I promise, the courts are going to ask for every receipt and record you can give them when the time comes.

Child support, parental alienation, and the other associated issues all tie back into physical custody. You have to catch this all upfront by ensuring your custody agreement includes these points:

1. **Equal overnight custody.** If for whatever reason you cannot have your kids half the time, ensure you know what you're really agreeing to and how that division will affect child support.

2. **Equal access.** Get your name on every list of "approved contacts," "listed guardians," or any other at any school, church, doctor's office, daycare, camps, and anything else your children are involved in.

3. **Specified location.** If you both live in a certain city, make that city the kids' "homebase" in the custody agreement. This way, your ex can't try to up and move them without your approval.

4. **Any other particularities.** Any other important aspects of your individual situation should be added into the custody agreement. For example, if you both agree to continue raising your children in a certain religion, get that in writing so it can't be backtracked.

Just because you want to include something in your custody agreement does not mean you'll actually get it. Sometimes you'll have to compromise in order to settle on a custody agreement. Other times, the courts can wear you down until you sign something anyways. The best way to set yourself up for a fair custody agreement with minimal contention is to do it all before you actually need it.

Again, discussing these possibilities with your partner and including them in your prenup is the #1 way to prevent *all* of these issues. While a prenup isn't foolproof, it does create a precedent. If your ex wants something completely different than what you'd previously agreed to, a prenup is something you can point back to.

A prenup is also extraordinarily important for setting the expectations of a co-parenting relationship. In an emotional and difficult situation, co-parenting *is* the best case scenario. It's in the best interests of everyone involved: you, your ex, and most importantly, your kids.

CHAPTER SEVEN

Co-Parenting

In any divorce or separation, co-parenting should *always* be the ultimate goal for everyone involved. Co-parenting is also a relatively new concept that's come out of the rise of divorces. Let's first define what exactly it is.

Co-parenting is a term that refers to a standing agreement between two parents to work together for the benefit of the children. The #1 focus of all co-parents is their children. The co-parents' relationship with each other is to put their children first and do what's best for them. It's as simple as that.

While it's nice to be on good terms with them, it doesn't mean that you have to be friends with your co-parent. You don't even have to *like* them. However, you both have to respect each other's roles. Respect is the foundation that a co-parenting relationship is built on.

When you can respect each other as equal figures in your childrens' lives and actively decide to co-parent, it's a whole different ball game. Instead of useless fights and years in court, you can all focus on establishing this new family dynamic and moving on with your lives. Co-parenting is the quickest and easiest way to get back on track.

No matter what, a divorce is going to impact your kids in some way. That's unfortunately inevitable here. But when the parents can maintain a good working relationship with each other, the impact on the kids is minimized as much as possible. They will have to adjust to the fact that Mom and Dad aren't together anymore, but co-parenting saves them from being in the middle of Mom and Dad's constant conflict. Instead of being "children of divorce," they can just focus on being kids.

Co-parenting is not only what's best for the kids; it's what's best for you, too. Here, you have a team player rather than an opponent. This is incredibly helpful in situations as small as picking the kids up from school when you're stuck at work to as significant as making healthcare decisions together. When you're both on the same page, it comes with so many intangible benefits that many wouldn't even realize.

As co-parents, you also have a lot more flexibility when it comes to custody and child support that a court would never allow for. This kind of flexibility is especially helpful for a high-value individual and not something you would ever get otherwise. When you are juggling a demanding career alongside your children, having a co-parent instead of an adversary makes life *so* much easier.

If you're constantly traveling or have fluctuating income, a co-parent will understand your situation and work with you to come up with something that makes sense for everyone. You might be on the road for Away Games while your co-parent goes to the same office every day, so they agree to let you have the kids during your off-season. Or, you might own a business that profits more in some quarters than others, and you and your co-parent decide a fair child support payment based on that particular revenue rather than a court order.

Court orders don't allow for any wiggle room and don't take specific situations into account. The court doesn't care that your mother's birthday isn't on "your" day, but a co-parent will be willing to trade days for those special events. Once you have your own agreement in place, the sky's the limit.

Co-parenting is to their benefit, too. When you aren't fighting for the basics, you are more than happy to pay for the extra things if you are able to. The majority of parents want to provide as much as they can for their kids, but the courts squeeze them out and eliminate that opportunity for parents to be able to do the extra stuff they'd really like to do otherwise.

This is why I believe that the biggest key to a co-parenting relationship is to *stay out of the courtroom as much as possible*. Involving the legal system will only drag this process out, and attorneys will only suck up money. The best way to establish this relationship is to stick to what you prenup outlined (if you have a prenup), create your own agreement, and put only the minimums on paper. You can always give additional support, but you don't want to have to be held to it no matter what.

There's no need to use the courts to come up with some cookie-cutter agreement if you can work together to do it instead. The less you can involve the legal system to establish your baseline, the more you and your co-parent will get out of the relationship both emotionally and financially.

Your document legal agreement does not have to be your actual agreement. What you have on paper should only be the bare minimum to avoid getting locked into something that you may not always be able to afford. Only documenting the minimum also allows you and your co-parent to make more decisions together. For example, your children may go to private school depending on where you live. That should be something that you can agree on together based on the current circumstances, not the courts. When a "sometimes" or "maybe" thing becomes mandated in the agreement, you both lose your ability to have a say.

Most parents will treat the documented minimum as just that—the minimum. They want to give their kids everything they have. And co-parents are not only happy to provide more, but they also feel more able to. If they had a good year at work, they aren't afraid to share that. They aren't worried that their ex will take them back to court to mandate more just because they can give more right now. Everything above the baseline can be discussed and adjusted as needed, but that conversation does not need to involve any attorneys. Co-parents can do that themselves.

Training for Game Day

As part of healthy communication, coparents may want to consider setting routine check-ins to review their current agreement and discuss whether they need adjustments. This could be as often as you both deem necessary, but a quarterly basis is generally best.

Figuring out your baseline and the agreement above it can be difficult if it wasn't already established in a prenup. Doing this during a divorce can be much more difficult--emotions are raw, tensions are high, and you may even struggle with anger or resentment toward each other. That's pretty common, after all. Many relationships don't end amicably, but that doesn't mean they can't create a good working relationship after.

You chose this person to be your partner, which didn't work out. In a childless marriage, you can often make a complete split and never talk to them again. However, you also chose this person to be the other parent of your children. This means your relationship can't really "end" in the sense of going no-contact forever the way others can. Instead, your relationship has evolved from spouses/partners to co-parents, and that relationship will last forever in some way, shape, or form.

You and your ex made the decision to bring another life (or lives) into the world, and that's a commitment that will never end. You will have to be in regular contact with your ex until your children have all turned eighteen at the very least. Even then, you'll still have to see them at family events. If you and your ex do not establish a healthy co-parenting relationship, important moments in your children's lives could be ruined by the tension between you two.

When your kid crosses the stage for graduation, do you want to be thinking about which parent will get to see them first after? What about when your children get married--do you want them to worry about keeping you and your ex apart during their wedding or when they have kids themselves?

Too many children of divorce have to deal with parents who can't even be in the same room together decades later. This strain can affect all aspects of both of your relationships with them for the rest of your lives. On the other hand, developing a healthy co-parenting relationship now will greatly ease tension both now and over time.

Remember, you are both actively choosing to become co-parents in order to do what's best for the kids. It doesn't matter why your marriage has come to an end or any of those past issues. If no criminal behavior was involved, then none of it matters anymore. As adults, it's your jobs to put aside your feelings and focus on your children.

The first step to moving past your past relationship and becoming co-parents is to recognize that your ex has just as big of a role and an impact in your children's lives, and you must respect each other as such. In a co-parenting relationship, there are actually three relationships at work: the business relationship between you and your co-parent, your relationship between you and your kids, and the relationship between your kids and your co-parent. The common goal should be to promote all three relationships.

As I've said, respecting each other and maintaining a relationship doesn't necessarily mean becoming friends. You can keep your communication strictly focused on the kids. However, respect means that you both need to be equal advocates of each other and support your children's relationship with the other parent. Instead of feeling "guilty" for wanting to spend time with the other, they should be encouraged. That is what healthy co-parenting is.

This is a two-way street. You need to do it just as much as your co-parent does. It's as simple as saying, "Hey, why don't I take you over to your dad's today to watch that football game?" or "It's Mother's Day. Why don't we go pick out some flowers for your mom?" These are very small acts that build up over time to help your children understand that they are not in the middle of a conflict and are free to develop two different, equally-connected relationships with you and your co-parent.

My ex was never supportive of my relationship with our boys. She never had any interest in becoming a coparent and actively undermined my attempts to foster a relationship with our children after the divorce. Being a victim of parental alienation like me is a nightmare in and of itself, but the biggest victims are the kids. Now, I have two grown sons who are not willing to develop a relationship in adulthood or even meet the rest of their family. I wish that things were different, but this is the unfortunate reality of the situation and I don't want anyone else to have to go through it. Opening the door to a coparenting relationship is one of the only ways to prevent this from happening to you and your children.

Stop and Think

Many people reading this book may be children of divorce themselves. Consider how your parents interacted with each other afterward. Did your parents develop a healthy co-parenting relationship?

If you're unsure, consider these questions:

- Did each parent encourage you to spend time with the other?
- How did your parents talk about each other?
- Are they able to be around each other now?
- As an adult, have you had to make special accommodations so that they do not interact with each other at special events?

Depending on your answers, it's possible they never established a healthy co-parenting relationship. Unfortunately, it may also mean that you do not have a good model of a co-parenting relationship in adulthood. It's important to be aware of these circumstances and its impact on you to avoid falling into an unhealthy co-parenting relationship.

Putting aside your personal relationship with your ex and remaining civil is most difficult in the beginning. Although it gets much easier as time goes on, you both may struggle to establish a co-parenting relationship while the emotions of your past relationship are still fresh. In these cases, a mediator may be recommended.

A mediator is an objective third-party who can help you both see the other's side and come to a fair agreement. There are mediators who work specifically with co-parents, so I highly recommend finding one with that particular experience to get the best possible outcome.

Mediation also only "works" when both parties are willing to come to the table. You and your ex may not be able to work out an agreement on your own, but you have to at least agree to use a mediator to do it. Co-parenting only happens when both parents agree to work together. If your ex isn't matching your efforts, then you unfortunately do not have a co-parent.

Beyond an initial mediator, counseling and therapy are great resources for co-parents to use at any point in their relationship. Like any relationship, co-parents can encounter occasional bumps as they work with each other to raise their children. A professional can help them sort out issues, strengthen their communication skills, and maintain their foundation of mutual respect.

Some people think that this kind of outside help means you can't "handle it" or is a sign of weakness, but that couldn't be more untrue. In fact, utilizing professional support is one of the smartest decisions you can make.

However, I would *highly* recommend that if you are both agreeing to therapy/counseling/etcetera of any frequency, don't include it in the documented legal agreement. Otherwise, it could become mandated at your expense.

Therapy is one of the many tools a high-value individual may need to use in order to balance every area of their hectic lives, both professionally and personally. You are attempting to navigate a difficult and complicated situation that you have likely never encountered before, but there are professionals whose entire expertise is in this field.

The fact that you are reading this book proves you are open-minded to the advice of others. In the next chapter, we'll talk about the various professionals you can bring into your corner for support so that you can continue to excel even through this situation.

CHAPTER EIGHT

In Your Corner

Everyone needs someone in their corner. The top pitcher in the MLB, the star linebacker in the NFL, and the best center in the NBA all have a team behind them to maintain peak performance—a coach, personal trainer, dietitian, and a range of other experts to help them behind the scenes. This is no different for successful people outside of sports, too. Business leaders and entrepreneurs are often backed by their accountants, bankers, lawyers, financial advisors, and others that aid them in reaching their big goals.

Many young athletes who are aspiring to go pro often don't realize just how many people it takes off the field to succeed on the field. I even founded my agency, Condition Sports Management, to help guide athletes as they progress in their career and maximize their earnings along the way. Whether an athlete is still in high school, playing at the college level, gone pro, or even transiting into their post-career life, one of the most important things they can do is to assemble a support team. Below is an example of what that team might look like.

The Athlete Support Roster

Personal Trainer: This is an expert who can tailor an off-field workout for your specific needs during the season and outside of it.

Flex Coach: They specifically work with you to increase your flexibility, which can help prevent injuries.

Dietician: This is an educated and licensed professional who can help create the best meal regimen to fuel your body and fulfill your personal macronutrient and vitamin requirements. Please note that a dietician and a nutritionist are not the same, as a dietician must complete much more education and training to obtain their license than a nutritionist.

Financial Advisor: Especially for young pros who are suddenly making a lot of money, a financial advisor can help you make the most responsible choices with your income and help set up your future.

Attorney: At the very least, it is a good idea to have an attorney on retainer to review all contracts you are presented with and help negotiate to get the most favorable terms.

Manager: An experienced manager can be the x-factor of the trajectory of your career. They can find new opportunities, advise you on important decisions, and guide you to success.

If you are a high-value individual or someone aspiring to be one, you need to build up a group of people to support you through your journey, *especially* when going through the trials of a divorce. Just like an athlete needs their team to take care of their physical health, you need a team to help you make the best decisions possible and ensure your emotional health as you undertake this mentally-taxing journey.

Some people can be very resistant to seeking outside help due to pride, ego, or misconceptions about who needs support. But the truth is that everyone needs support, and it doesn't make you any less of a person to admit that. The highest achievers and succeeders know how important it is to get the right people in their corner. In fact, their support helps guide them to success and continue to achieve. Your goals can be reached more quickly and with less stress when you have someone there to advise on each aspect of your life and career. Nobody can really do it on their own.

Your team should consist of experts who can assist and advise you with different aspects of your life. Their support can come in different ways at different times, depending on what you need at any given moment of your life. For a high-value individual going through a divorce, you should strongly consider adding the following list of members onto your team.

The Divorce Support Roster

Attorney: While this is a given for all legal matters, be sure to work with an attorney who is experienced in handling your situation and can help protect your assets. An attorney is ultimately working for the paycheck and likely won't look out for your best interests, but a good attorney is your best shot at a fair ruling in court and essential to include in your team.

Divorce Coach: This is someone who is highly knowledgeable in the process and can give you the guidance to get through it with the best outcome possible. I highly recommend finding someone like me who is a CDC Certified Divorce Coach to ensure they are qualified.

Mediator: When working with your ex to come to an agreement and establish a co-parenting relationship, a mediator can act as an emotional buffer and help you both see the other's side.

Therapist: They can help take care of a person's mental and emotional wellbeing throughout this period, as well as other points in their life.

Most of those experiencing a divorce immediately understand the value of an attorney and a mediator. Almost everyone who goes to court will employ legal representation and a mediator is commonly used to settle a dispute between two parties. However, there are a surprising number of people who are resistant to including a divorce coach and a therapist in their support team. Let's discuss.

If you are an athlete, you already have a coach and know how critical they are to bettering your game. A divorce coach provides the same value, albeit in a very different situation. We are highly knowledgeable, experienced, and, in some cases such as myself, it's personally happened to us and so we understand exactly what you are going through.

A divorce coach will walk you through everything to expect in a divorce and present all of your options throughout the process. They can advise you on how to handle every aspect of your divorce—agreements, alimony, child support, custody, and creating a co-parenting relationship—and point you to the right resources when needed. By utilizing a divorce coach, you can give yourself the best chance of having a "good" divorce with the most equitable outcome possible.

Most often, people will resist the suggestion of therapy for many reasons. They may think it is a waste of time, not applicable to their needs, or that it would somehow implicate a vulnerability. Like anything related to mental health, there are many popular misconceptions and fallacies that need to be dispelled.

There is a particular stigma surrounding emotional or mental support for men. Unfortunately, the subject of men's mental health has historically been treated poorly by society, and we still have a long way to go. There exist many outdated ideas of men being "weak" or "unmanly" if they seek any form of support. These ideas aren't just simply untrue, but they are also quite harmful and can prevent many men from getting help when they need it.

Kevin Love, the star player of the Cleveland Cavaliers, is notable for being one of the few male athletes to publicly speak about his lifelong struggle with anxiety and depression. He has said that therapy is "the best gift that you can give yourself" (Scipioni). While discussions on mental health have become more common and acceptable, many men still hesitate to open up because of the long-held stigmas.

Real-World Example

We all have a limit. At the 2020 Tokyo Olympics, one of the greatest gymnasts of all time withdrew from the Women's Individual All-Around Event due to mental health concerns. Living with ADHD and handling the everyday stress of a world-class athlete, she was overwhelmed by the pressure of the competition, the death of a loved one, and her upcoming testimony to the Senate in a hearing over the horrific sexual abuse that she and her teammates endured at the hands of their USA Gymnastics doctor, Larry Nassar. She had pushed herself too far and faced serious potential injuries if she continued. Her decision to withdraw was very controversial and she was criticized as a "quitter" by some media outlets, but her bravery to speak out has also sparked further discussion and destigmatization of mental health issues.

Even if you don't think you need any emotional support, it is still good to include that on your team in some form. You might be one of many people who think, *If I go to therapy, then that means I must have a problem.* This is another false idea associated with therapy. Seeing a therapist does not necessarily mean that you "need" to go or that you have some sort of mental problem to address. For many, therapy is a check-in as routine and uneventful as getting their oil changed.

Your support team should be built to cover everything about you. One part of you is your mental, emotional, and spiritual wellbeing. Regardless of whether you are actively going through a divorce or not, your psyche needs to be taken care of so that you can stay at the top of your game. A therapist is trained to assess how you're doing and make recommendations to improve or maintain your current emotional state. Therapy can look different for everyone, and it can be as frequently or occasionally as your situation calls for. It's just one more tool in your kit to keep you at the top of your game.

Therapy is especially useful during a divorce to help process the many associated emotions and mentally recover much quicker than you could on your own. They can often also hold sessions with you and your co-parent to make specific recommendations to improve the working relationship with you. Your children will also highly benefit from seeing a therapist to help them understand their feelings about the divorce and better acclimate to the new family dynamic. Really, everyone wins by seeing a therapist.

You are ultimately the one building this team and designing the program, and you can change it at any time. You retain complete control here. By creating a team and program to meet your specific needs, you make it that much easier to achieve all your goals. You only stand to benefit from doing this.

In the beginning, I recommend meeting with everyone on your team on a frequent basis while you establish the game plan. From there, you can determine how often you need to touch base with them based on your situation and what's going on in your life. This can be as many or as few times as you need. However, it's a good idea to check in on a quarterly basis at the very least to ensure you're always on track.

Again, this should all be done as soon as possible. If you are an aspiring athlete or have other big dreams, a support team will help you succeed. And if you are already at the top, your team will help keep you there. Sooner rather than later is always ideal, but later is better than never. If you haven't done it yet, there's no time like the present.

Regardless of when you decide to do this, a team can be formed at any stage of your life. It's especially helpful to do so before you even get married. Your partner is a key member on your team and it's important to agree on a game plan to avoid the most conflict possible.

To that end, premarital counseling can be an effective avenue to getting on the same page and develop your in-case-of agreements: what you'll do if you get a divorce, how your coparenting relationship will work, etcetera. While it's not so much the norm anymore, premarital counseling was often required by most churches to get married.

This is one thing of the past that I believe should have stayed in modern times. Premarital counseling is one of the best forms of preventative support to help couples establish a happy marriage and, if worse comes to worst, an amicable separation.

Training for Game Day

A premarital counselor is highly recommended for all of the aforementioned reasons. You can find a premarital counselor either through a religious leader, therapist, or another qualified professional. Be sure to find someone who is in line with your values and can act as an objective third-party.

When it comes to divorce and separation, the best offense is a good defense. If possible, it's much better to avoid the situation altogether. In the final chapter, we'll discuss protection and prevention tactics to keep you from becoming a target of the predatory divorce industry and other exploitation.

CHAPTER NINE

Don't Be a Target

As a high-value individual, you have a certain status and wealth that other people aspire toward. Some people will work hard to earn it for themselves, while some people scheme to take it from others. Since you have something that so many people want, you are *always* going to be a target to someone, somewhere, somehow. That's the unfortunate truth that you just have to accept.

Dealing with these predatory types of people simply comes with the territory. Depending on your area of success, you'll come across different types at different points of your life. Student athletes can start to see these people come out of the woodwork as early as high school, while aspiring doctors may not see them until they finish medical school. Sooner or later, though, they do show up in our lives and we have to identify and protect ourselves from them.

Once you have achieved success or it is clear that you imminently will, you'll notice that some people start to take a special interest in you. The "popular" kids who used to bully you suddenly want to be your friend now that you're getting recruited by multiple universities, girls or boys who didn't give you the time of day are calling you up for a date since your startup has taken off. Whoever they are, they have noticed you are doing well and want some sort of relationship with you as a result.

While this influx of attention can be quite flattering, you always have to stop and ask yourself: "Are they hanging out with me because they like *me*, or are they trying to *get* something from me?" It's not a fun question, but you have to answer it honestly.

Pausing and reflecting on this now can save you from significant loss and pain down the road.

High-value people tend to surround themselves with other high-value people for several reasons. One, these kinds of friends usually have similar lifestyles that align with your own and practice the same habits that made them successful. Two, those with status and wealth of their own are most likely not looking to profit off of yours. With this in mind, you unfortunately must be wary of those around you who are not successful in their own right, as they may introduce bad habits or value you only for what they can get.

At best, these status-chasers can be a negative influence and impede your success. Since they don't understand all the hard work it takes to get to where you're at or where you're going, they may try to convince you to blow off your responsibilities for short-term fun instead.

> "Missing one day of practice won't kill you. This party is going to be so fun!"

> "Still studying? Why don't you stop and play some video games instead?"

> "What's wrong with doing just one line? You're being a buzzkill."

This is a slippery slope that can lead you to falling off the path and bring you down to their level. And that's if they aren't actively trying to "get" anything out of you, either. When others know that you have something of value, these predators may try to manipulate you for their benefit. It could be as simple as asking to borrow money or help them get a job, or they could play a long and drawn-out game, which is much more dangerous.

This long-con more often happens with the "gold diggers" that we talked about at the start of this book. These women and men who romantically seek you out, get you to commit, and then take you for all you got in a divorce are a very real threat all high-value individuals face. By taking the necessary steps to protect yourself, you can hopefully avoid falling into this trap.

Now, I feel it's important to again state that being prepared for the worst-case scenarios does *not* mean you are "planning" for a divorce. It's like an athlete going to a flex coach to prevent an injury down the road. Does that mean they are planning to get injured during a game? Of course not, but this measure can help keep their careers from being cut short in case they do end up getting hurt on the field.

Nobody wants to contemplate their unexpected death or illness, but we all have life insurance for a reason. We are trying to maximize our worth so we don't lose any potential opportunities and since we can never 100% rule out the possibility of a marriage ending, you have to put some preventative measures in place so that this event does not derail your trajectory. Taking the opportunity to draw up all of your possible game plans now is how you can ensure the best outcome possible. Part of this prevention is thoroughly assessing whether your prospective long-term partner is really in it for the best intentions.

Nobody wants to look in the eyes of the person they want to spend the rest of their lives with and ask, "Do you love me, or do you love my money?" And you don't have to. Instead of openly questioning your partner, you just need to take the rose-tinted glasses off and watch out for common red flags.

Training for Game Day

Picking the right partner in life can make or break your continued ability to succeed. With that in mind, it's important to choose someone who will be by your side through the best and worst of times. To make sure they have the best of intentions, keep the following things in mind.

Timing. Did they know you before you "made it"? If so, why have they only expressed romantic interest now? This is usually more than just a coincidence.

Paying. When you go out, who is always picking up the check? Are you splitting the bill, or are you paying? Do they ever offer to pay for anything? Or do they ever offer to make dinner at home? Or, do they expect you to always pay their dinner bill even when you have been dating for an extended period of time? There might be a pattern here.

Pacing. How fast has the relationship been moving? Who is the one pushing to take things to the "next level"? If things are moving more quickly than normal, it's possible that they want to "lock it down" as soon as possible for a reason.

Prying. Do they ask questions about your finances beyond what's typical? It's one thing for a potential spouse to want to know whether you are in debt and your general economic status, but too many questions about exactly what you make and where are unusual.

Flaunting. Are they overly interested in "showing off" to others? Do you feel like they display you like a handbag or car? This could mean that they perceive you as a status symbol. If the way they treat you differs publicly and privately, there could be a problem.

One of the biggest things to watch out for is a track record. While we all have a history and should not necessarily be judged for our past, you should pay attention to any particular patterns with their prior relationships. For example, if they have had multiple failed marriages and have financially benefited from them, you may simply be the next target. Or if you are the latest in a string of doctors, lawyers, athletes, etcetera that they have dated, then they may be trying to "catch" one rather than form a genuine relationship with you. What they have done previously can sometimes be a strong predictor of what they will do in the future.

Beyond these red flags, it's really important to spend time with your prospective partner one-on-one in different situations so you can get a good idea of what life would be like with them. There are several things you absolutely need to know about your partner before you commit:

- Their lifestyle and beliefs, and whether they align with your own.
- Their life's plans, and whether they align with your own.
- What their parenting style would be, expectations on where to live, family time, etcetera.
- General tidiness and ability to coexist with other people in the same space.
- How they handle arguments, hardships, and other issues.
- How they manage their money, and whether they wish to merge finances.

These conversations can be difficult and uncomfortable to have, there's no doubt about that, but they need to be had. If your prospective partner balks at talking about "serious stuff" like this, then that's a huge sign that they may not be mature enough or ready for commitment. However, it can also be easier and more comfortable to foster these conversations in premarital counseling. I can't recommend a premarital counselor enough; they will help you to assess where you both stand on key issues, assess compatibility, identify potential issues, and improve communication to set you up for success.

Just like going to therapy, going to a premarital counselor doesn't mean that "something is wrong." If anything, it means that something is *right*—when you are both willing to work with an expert to establish your game plan, you have the best shot at a happy and long-lasting marriage. If your prospective partner is resistant to seeing a premarital counselor, then they may not really be on your team and you may need to reconsider your decision.

Utilizing a premarital counselor or a mediator alongside a lawyer is also helpful to create a detailed prenup that you both are happy to agree to. As we've already discussed, prenups are one of the best preventative measures that anyone can put in place, but it's important to get it done right. Make sure your prenup lists out everything relevant to your lives and futures—defined premarital assets, divorce settlements, co-parenting agreements, etcetera. And remember, a prenup can be thrown out the window in court, but having that document will set a powerful precedent and be your best chance of a good outcome.

But it doesn't stop there. Unlike the fairytales, you don't automatically get a "happy ever after" once you get married. Once that document has been signed, sealed, and delivered, you both still need to work together to affirm and maintain your partnership in life. At minimum, this means continuous communication and making an effort to spend one-on-one time with each other. While this may seem fairly obvious, these obligations are easily lost in the packed schedules of a high-value individual. Neglecting your partner, however unintentional, could come to kill the relationship if done for too long.

Since a high-value individual has more stressors and is generally busier than the average person, you may want to look into couple's counseling to prevent any breakdowns in the relationship. Remember, incorporating a qualified expert on your team can help you reach your goals faster while staying at the top of your game. Checking in with a counselor on whatever basis you and your partner decide is a great way to ensure you are both still communicating and connecting with each other.

As you and your partner progress in life, it's important to start setting routines and establishing certain customs in how you both operate within the partnership. Especially when it comes to finances and children, having certain norms already defined can make them harder to break in the event of a divorce. This baseline can also be a valuable gauge to show you whether or not your partner is continuing to be supportive and equitable in the relationship. Let's talk about what that baseline can look like.

If you are the breadwinner in the relationship, the division of bills is likely going to skew more toward you. And if you are already aware of and comfortable with that, that's okay. Many people pride themselves on their ability to support their families. Whether you want to pay for everything or establish some type of split, it's still very important to have that conversation with your partner well before you get married. If you find that your respective financial situations fluctuate or change in the course of your lives, a reevaluation will be needed. A supportive partner should be more than happy to sit down and do that with you.

Money is important, of course, but it's ultimately just a number. Your kids are the most important thing in your lives no matter what, and your top priority will shift completely to their wellbeing once they are born. This is true for any parent. And in a divorce, the matter of custody is almost always the #1 source of conflict, pain, and strife for everyone involved. While unfortunately this can't be completely prevented, establishing certain customs in your children's lives now is the best way to ensure that they will be carried on in a divorce.

This is especially important when it comes to family traditions and the division of holidays. Be aware of how much time with your children is split between your family and your partner's. If one side is clearly getting more time than the other, correct that as quickly as possible. Your children have two different sides of their family, and they need to get to know and form connections with both of them.

Before you even have children, you and your partner should decide how you will divide important holidays between your respective families and stick to that routine. If you've agreed to travel to your parents every other Christmas, then make sure you take that trip when you've said. By establishing and following these traditions now, they're more likely to "stick" and be written into custody agreements and so on.

If you are male, then it's especially important to ensure that your mother gets her special time with the children. Especially if you don't have any sisters, the paternal grandmother is usually dependent on her daughter-in-law to let her see her grandchildren. We all know how much grandparents dote on their grandchildren, so being denied that can be devastating to them. Agreeing on these times and traditions with your partner early on—and consistently following them—establishes a precedent for a custody agreement to adhere to, creates a balance of time spent with your two families, and ensures that all family members get to see the children. It's a win-win-win for everyone.

Stop and Think

If you are a child of divorce and estranged from one parent, are you still in touch with the rest of "that side"? Most likely, the answer is no.

The tragedy of parental alienation is not just that a child loses a relationship with their parent, but they also lose countless relationships with their extended family as well. My two sons have missed out on getting to know their grandparents and so many aunts, uncles, cousins, and other relatives who would welcome them with open arms. Family members beyond the parent almost always have no legal rights to see or visit with the child, so if the ex-partner has full custody and does not give access to the children, they will never get to know them.

If you do not want to reach out to your estranged parent, that is your choice. However, please consider reaching out to the grandparent, aunt, uncle, or cousin you never got to know. While forming that relationship in adulthood can be awkward, it's worth it to at least pick up the phone. They have likely been waiting in hope for your call.

Another thing to implement in your typical routine is recordkeeping. As we've already talked about, habitually indexing and storing receipts of things you've paid for could one day be incredibly helpful in proving your financial contributions in a divorce settlement. No attorney or judge is going to just take your word for it on what you are already paying for, so having the physical evidence is the only way to back up your claims. Trust me, it's much better to have and never need these receipts than to be left empty-handed in that worst-case scenario.

Recordkeeping isn't just about finances, though. In a divorce and custody case, you will need to show that you have already been financially supporting your family (so you aren't ordered to pay more than the minimum) and have an active role in your children's upbringing (so you are more likely to get your 50%). These records don't need to be meticulous—after all, none of us ever want to quantify our contributions as parents. Luckily, we don't have to. Accounting for time spent with your kids and what you do as a parent can be easily done just by marking stuff on a calendar.

For example, if you take your kids to their Saturday soccer games, then mark that down. If you pick them up from school every other day, mark that down. Call out of work to bring them to the doctor, mark that down. Any and all things you do with and for your kids, however small, should be noted in case you need a record later on. These seemingly meaningless things can become *very* important in a judge's custody decision, so you're better safe than sorry in this regard.

All of these preventative measures are relatively quick and simple to do, but they can make a *huge* difference in a divorce. While many divorces can be long foreseen and both parties have mutually agreed to end the marriage, others can seem like a complete surprise and blindside the individual. Whether it was a long time coming or out of the blue, you want to be prepared, and so you have to do your due diligence even if you think it truly will be until death do you part. As Benjamin Franklin said, "If you fail to plan, you are planning to fail," and it's much better to go to the trouble of enacting these preventative measures and never actually need them then to one day stand in court and lose your time, money, energy, and even your children.

The best way to protect yourself from exploitation is by avoiding becoming a target in the first place. By being cautious of who you let into your life and creating and keeping records of routines, you can prevent being targeted and maximize your potential.

Conclusion

As a high-value individual, you have invested a great deal of time and energy into yourself to get to where you are today. You have worked so hard, sacrificed so much, and grinded for so long to achieve what you have. This is why you are a high-value individual—you've made the effort that few others do to become successful. While your team has supported you along the way, you are ultimately the one who went out and did it. Your own abilities and willingness to persevere has led to wealth, status, and maybe even fame. You earned everything you have, and nobody should ever be able to take that away from you.

You are worth so much more than a check, but some people don't see it that way. Some people will specifically seek you out with the intent to take what is rightfully yours for themselves. And when money is on the table, the supposedly "just" legal system will throw ethics out the window. A vindictive ex is capable of doing terrible things, while attorneys only see dollar signs. You have no friends in a courtroom, and the only way to prevent the many potentially devastating outcomes is to be ready for it long before you ever walk in there.

Divorce can happen to anyone, and it can drastically affect your life if you are not prepared. The courts can drain your money, time, and energy—at best. A divorce can often cause career setbacks and severely impact your finances. And worst of all, you could lose your children to parental alienation, a tragedy that no parent should ever have to experience. This is why you have to contemplate the real possibility of your marriage ending and be prepared. There is simply too much at stake to ignore it.

This is why asset protection is so important. Taking preventative measures now is the only way to keep yourself safe and better the outcome of a potential divorce. It's also just one of the many tactics in your playbook to maximize your worth and realize your full potential. You can't let anything, not even a life-changing event, stop you from doing so. This is what it's all about.

Exiting a marriage should be as simple as it was to enter it, but unfortunately, the divorce industry has evolved to take every dollar possible. And as a high-value individual, you practically have a red bullseye on your back. You are inevitably a target, but you have worked too hard to let a divorce set you back. By using the tactics outlined in this book to protect yourself, you can save your money, time, energy and, most importantly, your children from being taken by an exploitative industry.

Glossary

Alimony: Court ordered financial support paid to an ex spouse. Also known as spousal support, it is an agreed upon amount of money to equalize the way that one was living during the marriage, either as a single payout or as recurring payments.

Alimony Clause: A legal clause found in prenuptial agreements stipulating that neither person is able to request or receive alimony in the case of a divorce

Asset: Resources with financial value that spouses can come into or acquire during a marriage. Depending on state laws, assets can vary between your property to your 401k. During the divorce process, time becomes a valuable asset.

Asset Protection: Preventative measures taken to protect valuables when entering a marriage, most often in the form of a prenuptial agreement.

Baby Trap: Getting pregnant to claim child support from a high-value individual.

Breadwinner: The parent who earns money to support the family.

Child Support: Payments made by a divorced parent to ensure an equal lifestyle for children split between coparents' homes. Often calculated by the duration of physical custody, the payments make sure that all of the children's needs are met: housing, food, healthcare, clothing, school supplies, etcetera.

Coparent: A parent that offers equal support to their children alongside their divorced spouse.

Coparenting: Offering equal access and an equal home for children between divorced parents. The relationship between coparents relies on healthy communication and puts the children first.

Coparenting Agreement: A standing agreement between two parents to work together for the benefit of the children.

Counselor: A qualified professional to mediate between partners, children, and divorced partners.

Covert Alienation: The process of a divorced parent subtly but deliberately isolating their children from the other coparent.

Custody: Parental rights and responsibilities to make decisions concerning a child's welfare as well as their physical residence.

Custody Battle: A legal fight between divorcing parents to claim the rights to raise their children.

Custody Division: A legal arrangement to split responsibilities and time with children between coparents. This does not necessarily mean that the split is equal.

Divorce: The legal termination of a marriage where the division of assets and child custody are negotiated either amicably or hostiley

Divorce Coach: An expert knowledgeable in the divorce process who can advise and support through each step of the proceedings.

Divorce Industry: The economic activity driven by divorces, worth up to $50 billion a year.

Divorce Proceedings: The legal processes necessary to dissolve a marriage in a court of law.

Divorce Support Team: A group of professionals to rely upon during a divorce. This includes attorneys, divorce coaches, mediators, and therapists.

Documented Agreement: The bare minimum requirements of a post-divorce arrangement recorded in legal documents. Having this baseline allows coparents flexibility in making decisions together.

Double Dipping: The practice of collecting from a divorce settlement and working in order to increase cash flow.

Equal Access: Comparable representation between coparents in all aspects of a child's life. This includes being listed as a parent at all activities and programs that a child is part of, from school to the doctor's office. This should be included in the custody agreement.

Estrangement: The tragic result of alienation in which a child of divorce loses relationships with their parent and extended family.

Ex: A former spouse or partner.

Exploitation: The act of unfairly misrepresenting a high-value individual during a divorce in order to gain an upper hand.

Gold Digger: A person who builds a relationship with a high-value individual to exploit them for financial gain.

Grandparent Alienation: As a parent pushes out a coparent from a child's life, the grandparents are simultaneously cut off from maintaining a positive and healthy relationship with their grandchildren.

Hearing: The presentation of evidence and testimony to the court in the decision making concerning custody, alimony, etcetera.

High-Value Individual: People who have accumulated a significant amount of wealth, fame, and/or status from advancing in their high-profile and high-paying careers.

Joint Custody: An agreement for equal control and time with a child between coparents.

Loss: The deprival of money, energy, time, or custody due to a divorce.

Marriage: The legal union of two people as partners in a relationship.

Mediation: Two parties working towards a fair agreement with an impartial third party as a guide.

Mediator: An objective third-party who can help divorcing spouses both see the other's side and come to a fair agreement.

Mental Health Stigma: An opinion of disgrace surrounding emotional or mental support, especially for men.

Overnights: Nights where your children stay over in your home. Courts will often determine custody division based on which parent has more overnights.

Parental Alienation: The process by which one parent allows and encourages a child's rejection of the other parent. By manipulating the child, the parent is able to gain more custody and control.

Parenting Time: The amount of time a child spends with each parent after they have separated.

Partner: Either member of a relationship or marriage.

Predator: A status-chaser who will try to manipulate high-value individuals for their own benefit, and be an overall bad influence.

Premarital Asset: Property and wealth one brings into a marriage. This should be defined in a prenup.

Premarital Counseling: Preventative support to help couples establish a healthy relationship before marriage and, if worse comes to worst, an amicable separation.

Prenup (Prenuptial Agreement): An agreement entered into by a couple before a marriage to determine how assets and custody will be divided should they separate.

Preventative Measure: Steps taken in advance of marriage for the possibility of divorce. This includes prenups, documentation, counseling, etcetera.

Reassessment: An evaluation for child support if a parent has a change in income.

Recordkeeping: An accounting of finances and time spent on a child's upbringing for a divorce and custody case.

Settlement: An agreement to finalize the terms of a divorce, usually including some form of payment and/or division of time for child custody.

State Laws: Rules depending on where a couple was married, divorced, and lived that can determine the outcome of a divorce.

Support Team: A group of professionals to rely on during the divorce process. This includes legal representation, a mediator, a divorce coach, or a therapist.

Target: A high-value individual whose wealth and status will draw the attention of predatory behavior.

Therapy: A tool of support to balance emotions and a hectic life especially before, during, and after a divorce.

50/50: An ideal, even split of child custody.

80%: The divorce rate within the NFL.

References

Bantock, Jack. "Simone Biles Says She 'Should Have Quit Way Before Tokyo'." CNN, 28 Sept. 2021, https://www.cnn.com/2021/09/28/sport/simone-biles-quit-tokyo-spt-intl/index.html

Boone, Christian. "Terrell Owens Pays Child Support, Avoids Jail Time." The Atlanta Journal-Constitution, 20 July 2012, https://www.ajc.com/news/local/terrell-owens-pays-child-support-avoids-jail-time/q3m0tk5vLYqXK3DAO8hnDM/

Boyles, Salynn. "Divorce Has Lasting Toll on Health." WebMD, 28 July 2009, https://www.webmd.com/balance/news/20090728/divorce-has-lasting-toll-on-health

"Do Marriage and Pro Athletes Mix?" ABC News, ABC News Network, 5 Jan. 2006, https://abcnews.go.com/2020/story?id=123669&page=1

"Drake Accused of Putting Hot Sauce in Condom & He Seemingly Responded on Instagram." Just Jared, 15 Jan. 2022, https://www.justjared.com/2022/01/15/drake-accused-of-putting-hot-sauce-in-condom-he-seemingly-responded-on-instagram/

Duncan, Judge Roderic. "How a Judge Decides the Alimony Amount." DivorceNet, NOLO, 19 Sept. 2018, https://www.divorcenet.com/resources/divorce-judge/how-judge-decides-alimony-amount.htm

Elsesser, Kim. "There Are More College-Educated Women than Men in the Workforce, but Women Still Lag behind Men in Pay." Forbes, Forbes Magazine, 3 July 2019, https://www.forbes.com/sites/kimelsesser/2019/07/02/now-theres-more-college-educated-women-than-men-in-workforce-but-women-still-lag-behind-men-in-pay/?sh=f6b7ee04c316

"Evander Holyfield's Mansion under Foreclosure." CNBC, AP, 5 Aug. 2010, https://www.cnbc.com/id/24998497

"FASTSTATS - Marriage and Divorce." Centers for Disease Control and Prevention, 4 May 2021, https://www.cdc.gov/nchs/fastats/marriage-divorce.htm

Hanf, Chuck. "Pro Athletes Should Just Say... 'I Don't' .... Marriage Can Wait." Bleacher Report, 12 Sept. 2017, https://bleacherreport.com/articles/234207-pro-athletes-should-just-say-i-dont-marriage-can-wait

Harris, Michael. "Brittany Renner Denies Trapping NBA Baller PJ Washington with Baby ." Rolling Out, 7 Nov. 2021, https://rollingout.com/2021/11/07/brittany-renner-denies-trapping-nba-baller-pj-washington-with-baby-video/

"How Much Does Divorce Cost in the USA." DivorceStatistics, https://www.divorcestatistics.info/how-much-does-divorce-cost-in-the-usa.html

Hughes, Dr. Carol R. "Why Is Divorce so Stressful?" Collaborative Divorce Solutions of Orange County, 22 June 2021, https://cdsoc.com/why-divorce-so-stressful-orange-county/

Kapos, Shia. "Kids Grown, Juanita Jordan Looks to Next Chapter." Chicago Business, 4 Nov. 2013, https://www.chicagobusiness.com/article/20131102/ISSUE09/311029978/juanita-jordan-ex-wife-of-basketball-legend-michael-jordan-speaks-out

McCullah, Karen. "Why Every Woman Should Get A Prenup." ELLE, 9 Jan. 2014, https://www.elle.com/life-love/sex-relationships/advice/a13998/why-every-woman-should-get-a-prenup/

Mitchell, Houston. "Wrestling Great Ric Flair Faces Arrest in Alimony Dispute." Los Angeles Times, 17 July 2013, https://www.latimes.com/sports/sportsnow/la-sp-sn-ric-flair-20130717-story.html

Owenby Law, P.A. "Statistics: Children & Divorce." Owenby Law, 25 Oct. 2018, https://www.owenbylaw.com/blog/2018/october/statistics-children-divorce/

Pelley, Virginia. "The Divorce Rate Is Different than You Think." Fatherly, 18 Feb. 2022, https://www.fatherly.com/love-money/what-is-divorce-rate-america/

S, Sitrus. "Failing to Plan Is Planning to Fail..." OrangeHRM, https://www.orangehrm.com/blog/failing-to-plan-is-planning-to-fail/

Scipioni, Jade. "NBA Star Kevin Love on Finding Success While Struggling with Mental Health: 'You Can't Achieve Yourself out of Depression.'" CNBC, 19 Nov. 2021, https://www.cnbc.com/2021/11/18/nba-star-kevin-love-on-mental-health-struggles-success-getting-covid.html

Von Boch-Galhau, Wilfred. "Parental Alienation (Syndrome) - A Serious Form of Child Psychological Abuse." Pubmed.gov, U.S. National Library of Medicine, 13 Apr. 2018, https://pubmed.ncbi.nlm.nih.gov/29654470/

WBNS-10TV Staff. "Florida Man Forced to Pay Child Support Despite DNA Test Proving He Is Not the Father." 10tv.Com, WBNS, 18 Oct. 2019, https://www.10tv.com/article/news/nation-world/florida-man-forced-pay-child-support-despite-dna-test-proving-he-not-father-2019-oct/530-9ae6c4e8-956f-4f86-b352-57db8df5ca44

"What Is Parental Alienation Syndrome?" Stop Abuse Campaign, https://stopabusecampaign.org/takeaction/family-court-custody-crisis/parental-alienation-syndrome/

Acknowledgements

*"If you want to go fast, go alone.
If you want to go far, go together."*

– African Proverb

I would like to express my sincere gratitude and thanks to the team of editors and illustrators who have worked with the Forever My Daddy publishing team. I would like to thank my mother, Rhonda, who continues to inspire me, motivate me, and express to me that there is still hope that one day my sons would want to have a relationship with me despite what feels to be a lifetime of effort.

I would like to acknowledge the special people who continue to support my efforts of unlimited projects towards eliminating parental alienation. Thank you, Robyn. You have always been supportive, attentive, and motivating. Your support has been unconditional. Thank you from the bottom of my heart.

Of course, I would like to thank my brother and father who have been supportive with unspoken words.

And just because...thank you Buren, Brian, Lloyd, Dante, Greg, Judy, Jeff, Yates, Esmer, SIL, Ty, JPaul, Justin, Jon, Reed, and Zachary.

www.ingramcontent.com/pod-product-compliance
Lightning Source LLC
Chambersburg PA
CBHW050323010526
44119CB00003B/75